Margaret Junkin Preston

Old Song and New

Margaret Junkin Preston

Old Song and New

ISBN/EAN: 9783744652841

Printed in Europe, USA, Canada, Australia, Japan

Cover: Foto ©Thomas Meinert / pixelio.de

More available books at **www.hansebooks.com**

OLD SONG AND NEW.

BY

MARGARET J. PRESTON.

───────

PHILADELPHIA
J. B. LIPPINCOTT & CO.
1870.

Entered according to Act of Congress, in the year 1870, by

J. B. LIPPINCOTT & CO.,

in the office of the Librarian of Congress, at Washington.

DEDICATION.

Day-duty done,—I've idled forth to get
   An hour's light pastime in the shady lanes,
   And here and there have pluckt with careless pains,
These wayside waifs,—sweet-brier and violet,
   And such like simple things that seemed indeed
   Flowers,—though perhaps, I knew not flower from weed.

What shall I do with them?—They find no place
   In stately vases where magnolias give
   Out sweets in which their faintness could not live:
Yet tied with grasses, posy-wise, for grace,
   I have no heart to cast them quite away,
   Though their brief bloom should not outlive the day.

Upon the open pages of your book,
   I lay them down:—And if within your eye
   A little tender mist I may descry,
Or a sweet sunshine flicker in your look,—
   Right happy will I be, though all declare
   No eye but love's could find a violet there.

CONTENTS.

FROM HEBREW STORY.

	PAGE
Ruth in the Land of Moab	15
The Daughter of the Gileadite	21
The Grief of Bathsheba	37
The Choice of Barzillai	40
Michal	44
The Royal Preacher	65
The Lament of Joab	69
The Writing of the King	72

FROM GREEK STORY.

Alcyoné	77
Erinna's Spinning	85
The Flight of Arethusa	90
Rhodopé's Sandal	94
The Quenched Brand	97

BALLAD AND OTHER VERSE.

The Lady Hildegarde's Wedding	109
Fra Angelico	114

CONTENTS.

	PAGE
The Nameless Pilgrim	118
The Dumb Poet	123
The Baby's Message	127
Attainment	130
The Signal	133
Unvisited	137
An Alpine Picture	140
The Color-Bearer	143
Nineteen	148
Wine on the Lees	151
A Year in Heaven	157
Afternoon	161
Poor Carlotta	164
The Complaint of Santa Claus	167
Unreason	170
The Legend of Athelney	172
All's Well	178
The Scholar's Haunts	180
Under the Elms	184
Antonio Oriboni	187
Artist-Work	191
Left Behind	197
The Bells of Brienne	200
Proem	203
Little Jeanie's Sleep	205
The Unattained	207
The Hallowed Name	209
Dante in Exile	211
The Vision of the Snow	214
Out of the Shadow	217
The Difference	220

CONTENTS.

	PAGE
Alone	222
Saint Cecilia	225
The Apostle of Truth	227
The Open Gate	229
The Resting-Place	232
The Rain-Drop's Fate	234
Rosalie	236
The Amulet	239
The Idle Lyre	240
Powers' Proserpine	242
Life-Close	244
The By-Gone	246
In Pace	249

SONNETS.

Equipoise	253
Saturday Night	254
Conviva Satur	255
The Morrow	256
Doubt	257
Ours	258
The Hyssop	259
Nature's Lesson	260
The Stirred Nest	261
The Reason	262
Undertow	263
If	264
Patience	265
The Shadow	266
Failure	267
Non Dolet	268

RELIGIOUS PIECES.

	PAGE
Rabboni	271
The Child Jesus	278
Supper at Bethany	282
Even so, Father	285
The Search of the Sages	289
The Young Ruler's Question	293
Ready	300
The Two Mites	302
The Sympathy of Jesus	305
The Little Pilgrims	308
Temple-Service	311

APOLOGY.

"What right hast *thou* to chirp?"—I asked a bird
    Whose slender trill I caught among the trees,
    Where thousands of full-throated harmonies
Pulsated on the undulant air, and stirred
The conscious forest-coverts, till I heard
    The leaves kiss, in their gladness,—while the breeze
    Broadened its wings to waft the melodies
Far up the west. The twitterer, at my word,
Paused:—(yet I missed no note:)—"Within the vale
    Are mates of mine,"—he piped—"for whom the lark
Soars with a song too distant,—yet who love
    My quiet cooings in the leafy dark:
For *them*,—not *thee*, I fill our nested grove;
Keep thou thine ear for lark and nightingale!"

FROM HEBREW STORY.

RUTH IN THE LAND OF MOAB.

I.

I sit apart bereaven,
Under the ashen shadows slant, with eyes
Too utter sorrowful to lift to heaven
So cruel-bright. Along the path that lies
Betwixt the fields of barley, to and fro,
The merry, careless folk do come and go,
Noisy with harvest mirth,—and I, so sad!
—I marvel, can it be
That ever I was light of heart or glad
As yonder maidens at the well I see
Filling their pitchers? Woe, ah, woe is me!
So bitter-sweet the memory of the day
We met beside the fountain,—he and I,—
And from my shoulder, or I framed reply,
He gat the urn, unheeding of my nay.
So long it seems, since I, as them, was gay,

Smiling at naught! Now o'er each water-jar,
Their veils thrown back, I watch them stoop to trace
    Their comeliness of face,
And laugh with pride to mark how fair they are.

II.

    Within the vineyards near
Shout the grape-gatherers, and amidst their cheer
Mingleth the hum of children,—ah, the pain!—
No more the dances of the harvest-time,
No more for me the vintage, fill the plain:
My clusters all are mildewed in their prime,—
My vine is clean uprooted; sun and rain,
Sharp and sore bitter in their mockery now,
Can call the living blossoms from my bough
    Never again!

III.

I watch the browsing flocks upon the hills,
And question of myself, if I but dreamed
What time we twain along the wimpling rills
Went hand in hand, he whiles, rehearsing tales
Of his young, innocent age, until, meseemed,
It he o'erlived in Judah's pleasant vales
Once more,—a ruddy boy in Bethlehem,
Shepherding there his father's happy herds:
And as, attent, I hung upon his words,
    Mindful alone of them,

As close and closer to his side I crept,
Half-unaware how marvellous-sweet it was,—
    Ceasing with sudden pause,
He oft-times lifted up his voice and wept,—
Yea, wept by reason of the joy he had,
And fell in tender-wise upon my breast,
Making my heart, with loving speech, right glad:
Anon he raised a heavenward hand and blest
The God of Jacob for His judgments sent,
Good wrought of evil,—out of death, fair life,
Famine and travail, loss and banishment,
    That gave him me to wife.

IV.

   Here on this wayside stone,
Alone as I had never been alone,
Had love not peopled these thrice-blessed years
With angels that made sweet the footed hours
Strewing the path I went, with thick-dropt flowers,—
I sit astonied—the harsh sackcloth spread
    Above my widow'd head,
And drink the wine and eat the bread of tears,
In utmost wrack and bitterness of mind
    That I am left behind.

V.

I see the olives ripening as of old;
The full-grown figs are yellowing in the sun;
The wheaten tassel deepens into gold,
   And all is just the same
To yonder reapers when the day is done,
   As if *he* went and came:
Who now doth weight the air with Chillion's name?
   —So must it be,—even so!
The over-jealous heart must yield, resigned
To know its dead forgotten, out of mind,—
Must learn, through grievous hurt, to hide the throe
Of wounded tenderness. Yon virgin band
Slow loitering still beside the fountain's curb,
Heedless as if no spoiler could disturb
Their light enchantments,—yet must feel the hand
Of doomed sorrow bow each head in turn;
Therefore I drop no wormwood in their wine:
Enough, if through the strength vouchsafed, they learn
To bear whatso of ill their lots assign,
   Unsharing aught of mine.

VI.

   Albeit of my distress
Acquaintance take light note,—yet I, indeed,
Grieve not therefor: 'tis no unkindly heed.
   Only one life the less

Counted among the kinsfolk; from the field
One sower missed;—amidst the vintage-cheer,
One merry, lacking voice, this harvest year,—
One arm the less the pruning-hook to wield,—
    And that is all,—is all,
Even to the friends that clave unto him well:
For me ... none other losses can befall:—
With him apart, so had I learned to dwell,
Hedged in a world that only held us twain,
Little it mattereth what may hence remain
Within the smitten, desolate wilderness
    Whereof *that life the less*
Made a Damascus garden for my soul.
O lost, lost love!—whose presence filled the whole
Of my full-laden life,—what marvel, I,
Emptied of thee, do rend my heart and die!

VII.

And yet,—and yet,—it hath no void, my soul:
It overflows as Jordan doth his marge
Wept flush by vernal floods that surge and roll,
Drowning the troubled pastures with surcharge
Of turbid waters. Empty? ... Grief is strong
To overcrowd the spirit even as love,
Leaving no verge for aught in heaven above,
Or in the earth beneath, it doth not throng
With its devouring gloom. Yea even, meseems,

The aching piteousness I keep for her,
The sad-eyed mother from whose forehead beams
Such hopeless patience, only is the stir
Of my pathetic memories. She was his,—
Of all, first kissed, first clung to. On her breast
The little head was nursed away to rest,
And therefore best I love her,—therefore 'tis
I cleave to her, the sole-left, human thing
For whom I yet entice myself to brave
The sting of living. Haply I might bring
Some medicament the bruiséd hurt to lave,
Some precious nard to soothe the lonely pain,
And reconcile her back to life again,—
That desolate path through which she fares to them,
Husband and sons,—a path behooven to be
Sad evermore. Now, empty-handed, she
     Returns to Bethlehem:
O joyless exile, what a woe is thine!
Can it out-mete the height and depth of mine?
—Then love shall lift the burden of that woe;
Whither thou goest, I will also go,
And where thou lodgest, there will I abide,
Thy people shall be mine,—thy God, my guide,—
Where thou dost die, there will I yield my breath,
And by thy side my burial-place shall be:
The Lord do so and more, if aught but death
     Part thee and me!

THE DAUGHTER OF THE GILEADITE.

I.

Through wage of war the pleasant land was waste;
The youth of Israel, man by man, had fallen,
Till all the valorous Leaders of the Tribes
Were counted among the slain. The hoary heads
Melted away like snow on Sannin's top,
By south winds smitten: and deliverance grew
A paling hope, as wore the days away.

Yet one stern lesson had the evil taught:
Astarté could not save; the priestly groves
Of Chemosh shrouded lying oracles;
The mystic star of Chiun forebore to shine:
Yea, furthermore,—when they had cried,—one ear
Only had heard,—one hand been stretcht to help;
And hence, in their sore straitness, they had turned
To seek in Urim and Thummim succor found
No other whither; and thenceforth they knew
The unimaged Yaveh for their one true God.

So came it then to pass that in their souls
Remembrance of the former time had place;

And ancient men made known how Canaan's kings,
From western border of Zidon, to the marge
Of Jordan eastward,—from the whiten'd crest
Of Hermon, set against the northern sky,
To the far reach of sandy Arabah,
Trembled before the Lord of Hosts, and fled.

Among the Elders sat there men whose sires
Were of the brave Three Hundred, who went forth
With Gideon, when he brake upon the camp
Of sleeping Midianites,—who spake and said,
Strengthening each other,—"Wherefore should we fail
Of such deliverance now? What lets that we
Call home our banished,—him we drave abroad,—
Restore the alien to his father's house,
Right whom we wronged, and cancel thus the wrong
By gift of leadership, that so he break
The yoke of bondage wherewithal we groan?"

Forth sped the clamor through the Tribes encamped
At Mizpeh;—"Call the banished home again!"
And ever and anon the cry arose,
Swelling and loudening with each day's acclaim,—
"Bring home the alien,—call the banished back!"

Then rose the Elders from the gates, and forth
They gat them over Jordan with their hest,

Saying:—"Come thou with us and be our Head;
Lead forth the Hosts, and take from this our hand
Due restitution for all wrong-doing past."

Then questioned Jephthah, counselling with his heart:
—"And wherefore not? Do I not tire betimes
Of this wild Lebanon's so narrow bourne,
And sigh for seemlier spoil than beasts of prey,
And other abiding-place than cloven crags?
I would have sovran empiry of men,—
I would have channel for the restless strength
That beats itself against these fastnesses:
And vengeance too,—vengeance so utter-keen
As pierceth sharper than a two-edg'd sword;
Vengeance that recompenseth years of wrong,
Not with forgiveness' stint,—that were too small;
But of such lordly bearing as wreaks itself
In blessings on the wrong-doer!—I will save
The land that cast me out,—a goodly land,
A land of ancient heroes, valorous men,—
Land of my father's sepulchre,—and of mine,—
Yea, verily, as my soul doth live,—of mine!"

II.

A thousand watch-fires shone on Mizpeh's slopes,
Where lay a mighty host of harness'd men
Waiting the morrow's march. The new-risen moon
Above the city swam in silences
Of infinite depth that mocked the innumerous stir
And tumult of the hour. Behind close walls
That hedged a garden, where a fountain's lapse
O'erbore the bruit of the uneasy camp,
And tempered the hot rush and tramp of feet
Along the ways, a maiden watched alone.
The air was rich with mingled spiceries,—
Citron and aloe, and all dew-drench'd sweets
That drowsed the night. Near by, a querulous dove,
Through broken dreams, made plaint,—till restless
     grown
Of bodeful echo to her own vext thought,
The maiden chiding turned, and heard the voice
Of him she had waited long,—"*Zanoné!—Thou!*"
And she made haste to answer, and right glad,
The twain sat down beneath the cassia trees,
And wist not if the cushat cooed or no.

Anon she drew the javelin from its belt,
And loosed the helmet's band: "Behold,"—she said,
"Thy locks are moist as never Amana's dews

Wet them, when thou hast lain night-long a-top:"
And in her hollowed palms she bare cool water,
And laved his brow therewith;—he answering:
—"Our life has purpose now to whet true toil,
That midst our rugged clefts it never knew;
And worthier aim than ravin of honeycombs,
Or branching antlers of the roe-buck slain,
Or leopard's spotted skin for warmth against
The biting hoar-frost"—

         "Yea,"—Zanoné spake,
Smoothing her finger on the weapon's edge,
—"This sharpen'd javelin hath brave work in hand,—
Its rightful end. Naught can it better essay
Than smite the heathen-folk that waste the land.
Such goodlier service have I craved for it,
Chafing against the woodcraft skill;—and now,
Sith that my wish hath answer fashioned to it
Above my hope,—wherefore ask I for more?
And yet—and yet, at whiles,"—

         But Aran laid
A hushing hand across the tender mouth,
Saying—"No word shall fill mine ear to-night
That is not freighted with a royal hope:
We needs must hoard all strengthening unguents up,
Wherewith to medicine heart-aches, while we shun
As baleful, every bitter herb of fear."

The maiden answered low:—"If he be lost
Amid the chance of war,—then what, to me,
Kinless, is left?"—"What left?" . . . and Aran spake
Wounded,—"O, naught,—naught left: for what am I,
Weighed in the balance of love, against a father!"
And from the light-girt waist the slacken'd arm
Slid down. A troubled glance Zanoné cast
Upon the averted face,—then sudden, sprang
Closer, and dropped her head upon his breast
And gave full way to a great gust of tears.
Whereat,—(by reason of one little drop
That held a honeyed bitter in its sweet,
—The wild-bee's sipping of the poison-cup,)
Came such a hurrying rush of passionate speech,
As heretofore, in her coy shamefastness,
She never had woven in words. And hearing it,
Aran could scarce repent him of his heat,
Seeing it wrought him largess, else unwon.

Then, after reconciliation had,
That made the love it quickened ten-fold sweeter,—
"Never before,"—he said—"saw I a fear
Whiten this cheek, or dim these steadfast eyes:
Or is it the blanching moon? Thus,—thus and thus—
I challenge the ruby back! Ha, now the glow,
Like the red lip of morn on Shenir's brow,
Chaseth the pallor hence. Lift thy dropt eyes,

—Dark, mountain-pools, as Jabbok's—with leave to mark
If yet their shaken depths be smooth enow
To mirror a stooping face." Thus squandering
Their one last hour in prodigal iterance
Of love's dear phases and vicissitudes,
(The tireless story that grew never old,
Though uttered and uttered o'er a thousand times,)
One hasted to them, saying,—"Behold,—my master
Would see his daughter ere he goeth hence."

They rose and followed. In the inner court
They found the Chief: and when at his command,
All had gone forth, Zanoné with swift step
Sprang to the arms that opened wide to her,
And fell upon the mailéd breast, and wept.

And Jephthah spake: "Approach, my son, and thus
Receive, ye twain, a blessing from my hand:"
Whereat, before the mighty man they knelt,
The maiden and the youth,—and in the name
Of Isaac's and Rebekah's God, he sought
For them a wedded life of joy and peace.

III.

The Hosts of Israel lay beside the fords
Of Jordan, tarrying for the embassies
That had gone forth to sue the Ammonite
With fair entreaty; and often as they sued,
Their message had been set at naught, till now
The people a-wearied of forbearance. Then,
And only then,—(for largest-natured souls
Be ever most long-suffering,)—did the Chief
Bid set the sacred standards forth, and fling
The blood-red banner abroad, by cunning hands
Of women broidered with the battle-call,—
"*The sword of Jephthah and of Gideon!*"

But ere they dipt their feet within the flood,
They lifted up with one accord, their voice,
And called upon the name of Israel's God.
Before the altar ministered ancient priests,
Who prayed the Lord of Hosts to lead them forth,
Scatter the heathen, break their bow of strength,
And give the victory. Jephthah heard, deep-moved;
A holy jealousy wrought in his soul;
The in-bred loyalty of long-gone years
Brake through the barriers exile heaped erewhile,
A headlong torrent, that swept clean away
All wreck of bitterness,—all choking gorge

Thitherward tided by the surging past,—
And in the tumult of his hurrying zeal,
With his right hand up-lift before the Lord
He sware:—
    "If Thou deliver our enemies
Up to my sword until they be destroyed,
Even to the uttermost,—then shall it be
That whatsoever cometh from my doors
To meet me, when I do return in peace,
Shall be a whole burnt-offering to the Lord."

Up rose the solemn smoke of sacrifice,
Bearing, with rich frankincense consecrate,
The vow to heaven. The mitred priests bent low;
The people shouted with the clash of arms,
"Amen,—Amen! So let it be!"

IV.

   —Strange mirth
Once more went smiling through the long-waste land;
And hearts that scarce had ever known a joy,
Lifted, as lifts the heavy-headed grain

At tidings of the coming of the wind.
The ancient men for whom all hope had ashened
Into the piteousness of gray despair
That nursed no ember of better days to be,—
Through gladness rent their garments: For had not
    God
In very deed made bare His mighty arm,
And given the evil haters of His name
Into His servant's hand?
                        —The wide-spread plains
Of Ammon ran with slaughter: Twenty towns
Unbarred their gates before the conqueror:
Rabbah had fallen:—the "City of the Waters,"—
Minnith was taken; widow'd Aroër
Sat desolate, because her sons were slain.

With songs of triumph,—trumpets braying loud,
Victorious standards borne aloft,—sheath'd swords
Girt on their thighs,—hackt bucklers loosened off,
And heads unhelmeted,—the avenging hosts
Stood on the Jordan's nether shore again,
And all, as with strong wine, were drunk with joy.
Now might the fields their seeded increase yield,—
The reaper bind his sheaves, safe-girt from harm,—
The vineyard-clusters ripen as of old,
And merry tumult fill the olive-groves
Once more: For all the land had rest from war.

Along the march forth came the Hebrew women
With solemn dances and ascriptive praise.
And wilder, as the leagues still lessened, grew
The gladsomeness, till even the piney hills
Were moved to laughter, and the trees clapt hands.

"*Mizpeh!*—The Lord *hath* watched betwixt his own,
And brought us back in peace:"—and Aran sought
The eye of Jephthah, as who should reply;
But Jephthah answered not, nor lifted up
His face to welcome Mizpeh's towers that shone
Fair on the horizon's edge. When lo! a clash
Of timbrels swam athwart the grassy slopes,
And silvery voices rose and fell and died;
Then clearer, nearer swelled most jubilant
With question and response.
    . . . A quick white flutter
Of womanly vesture,—eager arms outstretcht,—
Unfilleted locks against his breastplate flung,—
Wide eyes, whereof the heaven was dashed with
  tears,—
Pale-parted lips struck dumb through rush of bliss,—
He saw,—he knew,—and from the stricken heart
Of the stout mailéd warrior, burst there forth
A mighty and exceeding bitter cry;
"My child!—My daughter!—Woe is me—my child!"

V.

"She doth not ask,—my lamb of sacrifice,
She will not suffer remission of my vow:
And I,—Yea, I have sworn before the Lord,
And who may disannul? O hateful pride!
Maddest ambition!—most accursed greed,
That thought to bribe Heaven thus, and so to be
Accepted thus! Would God that I had died
An alien,—seeing my native land no more!
Would God, some bow, at venture drawn, had slain me,
And I had never beholden her face again!

"My tender dove,—my one sweet comforter,—
Laid youngling on mine empty heart, that else
Had crazed and broken itself above my dead!
And day-long, how she close and closer crept
Into the darken'd, shivering, frozen void,
Till it waxed warm, anon, with human love!
How hath she cheered my cruel banishment,—
Mossed the sharp flints with soft observances,—
Made of my goat-skin tent a pastoral home,—
Soothed when I chode, and kept within my soul
The wholesome fear of God! How did her wiles
Cheat me of ruth, and win me oft aside
From vengeful aims and angry discontents;—
And this,—ah, woe!—*is* this the end of all?

"Zanoné,—my one child!—I thought to see
Thee stand at Aran's side, an honored wife,—
To lift my head and proudly say,—'My son!'
And count the easeful, happy years go by,
When thy fair boys, like oaks on Lebanon,
Should overtop thy height,—alas, the day!
The strong man's arm is as a stubble-stalk,
And his stout will, as a bowed bulrush, yields.
My spirit is smitten: How can I give thee up,
My beautiful? Thou God of Abraham,
Wilt Thou naught else?—Is there none other victim?
No hallowed firstling on whose innocent head
I dare devolve my vow, and hear Thee say,
'Lo I accept thy ransom?' Thou art strong,
And I am weak:—O, woe is me!—my child!"

VI.

The weeks of wail had worn unto their verge;
And now within a grove of cypress glooms,
Apart from the companions of her woe,
Zanoné stood,—fixéd and white,—fast held
With stress of agony in Aran's arms.

The sun athwart them shed his setting gleams,
Red as the sacrificial flame;—his gleams
Whose latest must mark their hour of parting come.
By reason of anguish was the youth's strong frame
Shrunken; his tongue essayed delirious words,
Wild, void of meaning and direful. But for her,
The vestal in her consecrated calm,
Over whose soul the swallowing sea had gone
And left her wrecked of all, save awestruck faith
And love that overleaps the grave,—the strife
Was ended. On her straitened lips, a smile
Saintly as death's, lingered as loth to go:
Light, strange, ineffable, shone in her eyes
Like the Shekinah's glory; and her words
Came loftily, with firm, unbroken voice,
As Miriam's song on the red shore of triumph.
"Now we let go for ever earthly hands,—
Now tear our twinéd souls apart, and hence
Look to the meeting in the Canaan yonder!
O love,—make sure of this:—Dost thou not know
That fatherly pity filleth the Highest's heart?
Then learn it from me: In silence of the night,
Among the reaches of these mournful vales,
A spirit bare inward to my listening sense
This heaven-sent truth:—'Ye do not part for aye:'
By it I hold for solace in my woe:
Do thou likewise the same. Cling to that faith,—

Bind it, beseech thee, o'er the fiery pain
That else will burn thy tender heart to ashes.

"And now my soul doth lift itself to bless
Thy crowning love,—love that hath given to me
Sovereignty dearer than a sceptred queen's.
O strangest, sweetest love!—O bitterest love!
I die to think on it:—no more,—no more!
No backward look! Yet know thou, for a truth,
That in my Holy of Holies, Memory
Hath laid up in her golden manna-pot
Our earthly loves,—unwasting, pure for ever!

"I dare not weep: I find no place for tears:
I am the accepted sacrifice to God,
Devoted, set apart henceforth to Him.
Promoted to such honor, who am I
To murmur at the costly offering?
I save my country: Thou would'st dare the death—
Yea, thou *hast* dared it, facing of the foe,
For such a reason full oft. My poor, lost name!
Let it not perish out of Israel:
But when the land is rich in peaceful homes,
And blessedness of husband, wife and child,
Would they might keep some mindfulness of one
Whose hopes were all foregone! Would they might
    teach,—

These happy mothers—teach their little ones,
With pitiful lips to say it,—'*Poor Zanoné!*'
And O my father! But thou wilt be both,
Daughter and son to him, yea, twain in one;
The strength, the will to shield,—that shall be thine,
The watchfulness of unforgetting love
That never sleeps,—that shall be mine,—through thee.

"Behold,—behold! The latest reddening ray
Ashens behind yon Gileaditish hills,—
Those peaceful, peaceful hills!—O love, my love!
So! . . . let me crowd the travail of my soul
Into this kiss,—divinest of my life;
And kneel thou, while I lay on thy dear head
Once more my hands,—this once, once more—and
    pray:
Jehovah bless and keep thee: The Lord God
Be very gracious unto thee,—lift up
On thee His glorious countenance, Belovéd,
And give thee peace."

THE GRIEF OF BATHSHEBA.

I.

My little one,—my innocent nursing child,
That wottest not of evil!—that hast been
Thy mother's one requital in her sin,
Making it tolerable,—my undefiled,
Must *thou* die *for* me? O my God, my God!
Since mine the trespass, mine the suffering too!
           Lay Thou Thy rod
Of righteous scourging on my guilty flesh,
Till my transgression tortures me anew,
And all my half-healed wounds do bleed afresh:
But spare,—Thou Just One!—spare this guiltless lamb
Who crazeth me with his perpléxéd eyes,
That question,—"Wherefore thus?" Behold, *I* am
Sole cause and sore, my spotless sacrifice!

II.

        —The same,—ah me! the same,—
That piteous, helpless, mute-appealing look,
That oft hath sent a shudder through my frame,
When to the brazen altar-foot I took

A kid for my oblation. Can I lay
Naught on that altar now that will suffice?
Are flocks of Kedar vain to wash away
The shame I weep for? Is there other price
Wherewith my soul may purchase its release,
        And go in peace,
Cleansed, pardoned and accepted, O Most High?
        —Or must I bring
This one-year suckling as sin-offering?
Nay, then,—far rather, dying, let me die!

III.

        —How could I dare
To lift in Paradise, mine eyes to his,
If he, mine unoffending one, were 'ware
That she who held God's place to him,—through this
Her bitter wrong, had robbed him of the throne,—
My princely child,—that else had been his own?

IV.

        —If I might only die
In thy soul's stead, and thou, unhurt go free!
O prayer, how vain!—the lot hath fallen on thee:
Yet might the grief be borne, methinks, if I
Could hear thy wordless tongue once frame *"forgiven:"*

But if not here,—not here,
It falleth ever on mine aching ear,
Speak *that* word, first of all, to me in heaven!

v.

Mine innocent, baby-child,—
It grieves thy lip to mark my look of woe:
Thou canst not know it here, thou need'st not know
Wherefore thy mother's mouth so seldom smiled.
She knew thou wast but lent; *that* word was sure:
And never across thy rounded cheek hath passed
An ivory pallor, though it might endure
The fleetest moment, but a molten fear
Caught at her heart,—"the hour—the hour, at last!"
Yet when I looked not for it, it was here;
Yea—it *is* here!—Behold . . .
His fingers tighten . . . See, I cannot wring
Mine from their clasp;—his forehead is a-cold,—
The King,—haste, fetch the King!

THE CHOICE OF BARZILLAI.

I.

Now blessèd be for evermore
   The God of Jacob, who hath turned
   Aside the jealous wrath that burned
Against our Lord the King, and o'er
The plotters of his fall hath poured
   His awful vengeance like a flame
   Of all-devouring fire;—His name
Who wrought deliverance, be adored!

II.

But humble with no gifts' reward,
   Thy servant for light favor lent,
   In this the grievous banishment
Wherewith the abjects vex my lord.
I did but offer bread and wine,
And slaughtered sheep and milk of kine,
   Of my abundance, to the host
Fainting for lack of meat. Bestow,
   Beseech thee, that I crave the most,—
Thy royal blessing ere thou go.

III.

Nor seek not I should turn aside
   From these my fathers' ancient fields,
   The land that store of plenty yields,
The pastures where my flocks abide,
The jagged rocks along whose edge
   My youth hath chased the wild-goat oft,
These vales within whose reedy sedge
   I've heard the turtle cooing soft:—

IV.

The tents where dear my kindred dwell,
   The brook whereof athirst I drank,
   And made my bed upon its bank;
The coolness of yon shaded well,
   Where, at the noontide's waxing hot,
We drave the herds for watering;
It seemeth but a little thing,
   Yet, good my Lord,—entreat me not!

V.

Thy servant hath no heart to cross
   This Jordan; brief and evil be
   The days laid up in store for me,
And what account were gain or loss?
Life weareth to its bourne, and I,
   Infirm of step, beset by fears,

And with the weight of fourscore years
Burdened and bent, draw near to die.

VI.

To senses that be dulled or dead,
   Or can discern nor good nor ill,
   Though fair I know my Gilead still,—
Doth aught avail of fairness spread?
What now to me the dainty meats?
   What Mahanäïm's choicest wine,
   Or baskets heaped from Sibmah's vine,
Or far Rogélim's gathered sweets?

VII.

Within the porches of mine ear,
   The voice of singing-women throngs
   Confusedly. Even though I trod
The sacred courts, and stood a-near
   Within the holy hill of God,—
   The altar services, the songs,
The chanting priests I should not hear.

VIII.

Then let thy servant find, I pray,
   Grace in thy sight, nor seek to bring
   A burdening charge upon the King,
And get thou on thy royal way.

Among my kindred have I dwelt,
  Among my kindred would I die,
  With ancient neighbors waiting nigh,
Whose heart with year-long grief will melt.
My people's sepulchres I crave
  For burial-place: I would be laid
  By the lign-aloe trees that shade
My father's and my mother's grave.

MICHAL.

I.

NAAMAH.

Sweet Princess,—shadows on thy brow again?
We, thy companions, sigh to see thee sad.

MICHAL.

Have I not reason? Mark yon purple blot
Of darkness dropt upon the summer blue
Of Ephraim's peak; thereby thou well mayst know,
Sparing an upward look, that overhead
Drifteth a cloud. Even so upon my spirit
Lieth the blotting shadow. Thou hast heard,—

NAAMAH.

Yea, somewhat: but beseech thee, stay thy heart;
As heretofore, the dæmon will pass away.

MICHAL.

Would I dare venture where he broods withdrawn,

Amazed and dumb, within the shuddering dark,
And make him know the touch of helpful hands,
And speak some word for soothing,—my dear father!

NAAMAH.

It were not best;—pray thee put by the thought:
For stouter hearts than thine have shrunk to mark
The inward throes by which his strength is shorn.

MICHAL.

He beareth all the people on his heart,
And needs must stagger with the mighty weight:
The coil of sovereignty doth bind his brows
So straitly they are crazed; for I do hold
No memory of such evil moods what time
We dwelt in pastoral peace among the hills.

NAAMAH.

What marvel war hath overwrought him thus?
The hungriest lion on Bethalga's steep
Crouching to watch the folds, were sportive prey
Beside this Zobah and these heathen Kings,
And all the swarming Children of the East.
Yet better so than the obscure estate,—
The grapple with the fiend,—so power be in it,
Than levels of sultry calm. Thinks't thou not so?

MICHAL.

Nay, verily!—For oft at sunset-tide,
When maidens, poising on their happy heads
Their baskets reddened with the bleeding grapes,
Come trooping home; or when at dawn I catch
The early whistle of the harvest-lads
Among the barley-swathes,—how the old times
With longing seize me, and I pine to reave
Aside these gauds that overmuch oppress,
And be that blithest of human things, a child!
Such joy it was to dance with all the rest,
No dignities disallowing, midst the vines;
To frolic with the kids at folding-time,
To tumble the stretcht linen's bleaching webs,
Or with my brothers shred the olives down,
Or follow where the shepherds led the flock
To browse upon the aftermath. No songs,
No laughter now, no mirthfulness, methinks,
Rings with a tittle of the dizzy joy
My childhood knew. And yet I own, withal,
Amends,—marking my father's topping height
As royally tower amid the Tribes as ever
Aforetime in our little Benjamin:
Albeit for love of him, my soul is sad.
One told how minstrelsy had chased his gloom;
Whence came the singer?

NAAMAH.

He is one of those
Searched out for his good gifts, by the lord Abner;
Well skilled to twist the melodies perplext
Among the harp-strings, into fibrous chants
That draw men's souls out—

MICHAL.

Would he held the power
To bid the spirit of evil shrink abashed,
As ghosts at touch of dawn:

NAAMAH.

Ay, verily,
'Tis said he hath such charm—

MICHAL.

As spirits obey?
A spell to fright the fiend?—O better far
Than rarest skill of shepherd's reedy craft!

NAAMAH.

Yea, both are his,—the strength, the sweetness also.
Would that thy listening ear, three days agone,
Had heard the Virgin-song,—the 'Alamoth,'
Whose fluty richness ravishes the sense
Like quick, thick bird-notes dropt straight out of heaven!

Or that devout and holy cantillation
That caused the thunder-rack on the King's brow
To empty itself in tears, whereof the flow
Made all his shriveling powers up-lift—

Michal.

    —Thou, then
Hast heard the stripling?

Naamah.

    Stripling!—he is tall
Even as thy princely brother, and his face
Hath the clear splendor of the breaking morn.
Methinks amid the youths of Israel,
For comeliness, no form can mate with his;
And in his sheathéd eye is covert fire,
That only waits the breath of sacred song,
To make it gleam as Samuel's, when at Ramah
He prophesies before the Oracle.

Michal.

Thy over-praise hath stirred a wish to know
Whence comes the secret of this marvelous player.

Naamah.

And wherefore not? It may be easy compassed:
Behind the curtains thou mayst sit unseen,

And so make proof, when next the King doth call him,
Even for thyself, of this his mastership.

II.

SAUL.

Not yet,—my soul not yet hath clean escaped
The pangs wherewith the fiend hath holden me clutched:
Abner, attest me,—witness that my spirit
Never hath cowered before a mortal foe;
Of old thou so hast often proven it—

ABNER.

    Yea,
My Lord, O King; the arm of Joshua struck
None mightier blows at Ajalon than thine
Hath dealt to Amalek till he is destroyed.
What canst thou more? Thy latest enemy
Yields, vanquished now.

SAUL.

    —The latest?—nay, the latest
Here in my breast wageth such perilous strife
That I am shamed, and crave thy testimony
That not the terrible hordes of Philistines
Stinging like madden'd bees, prevailed against me

As thou hast seen the speechless terror prevail
What time the abhorréd dæmon buffeted.

ABNER.

My Lord, thou ever hast gotten the victory;
And even now the look of kingship comes
Back to thy brow, just as aforetime.

SAUL.

Nay—
This loathéd gloom—it hangs about my strength
And drags me down, as once on shaggy Seir
A lion's whelp sprang on me from his lair,
Amid so swart a darkness I could find
Naught of the weapons ungirded from my side.
Would God 'twere only as a lion's whelp!
My boasted strength! Behold this shrunken arm,
That once could dent the seven-fold bosséd shield,
Or snap a bundle of ashen spears like straw,
Or hold the unbridled colt in wildest plunge,
Behold it now with unaverted face.
But nay,—I scorn thy pity. O, my friend,
Thou darest not pity! And yet the man who never
Before stark flesh hath quailed,—whose steel-like thews
Have craved the joy of peril,—may unashamed
Shiver when spirits do brave him.

ABNER.
Pray thee bid
Into thy presence, O King, the youth whose song
At other times hath wrought deliverance
When thou wert vext and sore distraught of soul.

SAUL.
The lad whose hale, wind-brighten'd face hath in it
The morning crispness of Mount Ephraim?
Nay . . . As thou wilt . . . I care not: what avails?

DAVID ENTERS.
Look ye,—I am o'erworn,—ready to perish
For lack of that thou keepest a surfeit of,
Heart-quiet, untroubled peace: Boy, at thy peril,
Rant not of battle-fields, nor warriors' shouts,
Nor aught that hints the turbulence of life:
Away with these! Give me some cricket-chirp,
Or creak of wain, or beat of busy flail,—
Aught that will deaden the viper's hiss:—dost hear?

DAVID SINGS.

I.
Mine eyes I will lift to the hills
          Whence cometh mine aid;
The Lord all my counsel fulfils,
  Who the earth and the heavens hath made.

II.

No whither thy footsteps shall go
                      But still He will keep;
The watcher of Israel,—lo!
   He neither shall slumber nor sleep.

III.

The Lord is thy shade—is thy stay,
                      On thy left hand, thy right;
The sun shall not smite thee by day,
   The moon shall not hurt thee by night.

IV.

The Lord shall preserve thee from ill,
                      Thy comforts restore:
—Out-going and in-coming, He will
   Uphold thee henceforth evermore!

Saul.

Hath the boy magic hidden in his touch?
Abner, the reaching voice, like a cool hand,
Gropes through the smothering darkness,—feels for mine,
And leads me back,—back to the bleat of lambs,
And lowing herds among the thymy hills;
The beautiful hills from whence doth come mine aid!
Ha, the air clears: I draw free breath again,

As if I clomb some farthest misty peak,
And gazed sheer downward to the Hinder Sea:
My happy hills!—my calm, perpetual hills!
Lo, the old fervor surges through my soul;
I am the Lord's anointed: Verily,
As my soul liveth, I do feel the might
That took my spirit, whenas at Tabor's foot
I felt the prophet's in-breathed mystery.
Haste,—bid my servants bring my mightiest sword
Glittering and sharp, and gird it on my thigh:
Over my shoulders lay the lordly robe
And let me walk abroad in sight of men,
And make them know me for a King once more!

III.

Michal.

—Comely to see; ay, she did speak true words,
The garrulous girl; for never in Benjamin
Saw I his mate for stately-statured grace:
That up-lift brow, white as a cygnet's breast;
That stag-like mien, erect before the King
As he were royal too; that tameless port,
So unafraid, yet sweet with courteousness

Born only of courts: How could I deem him bred
Obscure among the sheep-cotes? Ah, my pride!
He might make answer,—' Have thou care, my princess,
Or ere I challenge thy count of dynasties
That lose their reckoning in the far-off Kish!'
—Merab, my sister, did she hear my taunt,
Would frown reproof on such disloyalty.
To her, the state: to me the memories,
The simple memories, of my simple life,—
Of conies hunted in the new-reaped fields,
Of gamesome hidings on the threshing-floors,
And all the pleasance of the harvest-feast:
O joys too full!—beyond a princess' reach!

Those tender canticles! Their breath is sweet
As odors of the evening-sacrifice:
They bore me up, as when the Prophet's voice
Before the door-place of the Tabernacle
Uttereth the solemn benediction. Yet
This voice that hath a lapse as Kishon's flow,
And whisperings softer than Beth-nimrah's reeds,
Hides slumbering mastery in its unused power.
The peaceful shepherd's staff and scrip . . . Go to!
Helmet and spear and shield for such as he!
The King doth love him; he will come to honor;
Naught lacketh he save opportunity;
And opportunity, to noble souls,

Is but fair leave to flower the golden core
Of nature out; and peradventure such
The shiftings of these troublous times may fetch him.

IV.

Naamah.

Who goeth forth,—so runneth the proclamation,—
To meet this Canaanitish champion,
And in the fateful combat overcomes,
Shall have to wife the daughter of the King,
His eldest born—

Michal.

   O, bless thee for the word,—
His *eldest!* Joy I pray it bear my sister,
If haply one among the valiantest
Of Heads of Tribes in Judah dares the proof
For getting of such guerdon.

Naamah.

   Nay, I wot of
Some fairer-faced, of whom the approving smile

Should be the tempting crown held forth to bind
Right fittingly the brows of high endeavor.

Michal.

An archer's lure! I tell thee I hold my state
A sanctuary,—not a guardless target set
Whereby to wage and measure trial of skill.
Commend my sister to the feathered chance,
And God forfend, no son of Belial win,—
As well may hap,—out-arrowing all the Princes!
For who that farthest tracks the ravening wolves,
(Nurtured in danger on rough mountain-sides)
The hunter of the iron hand and heart,
—Why seest thou not how such may bear away
The lily-wreath upon his spear's point, rather
Than one of the great lords? Out on the bribe!
'Tis all unworthy of my noble father.

Naamah.

Beseech thee grace; and yet, meseems, thou ratest
Too low the prowess of our royal Tribes,
Matching their well-proven nobleness against
Such bulls of Bashan. Think'st thou not, defiance
Like this must needs arouse the princeliest
And fire their souls with wrathful emulation?
Only fine natures nurse the great resolve,
And dare all peril for safety of the right.

That chrysopras upon thy jewel'd wrist,
On its clear surface holds the signet fast,
Which never Egyptian lapidary cut,
With all his craft, thus sharp on common amber.
The tallest palms bear ever the delicate dates:
Fruited pomegranates stand, the brambles crawl.

Michal.

Well, be she free, my sister,—free to risk
Signet of amber, or wild tamarisks;
No let would I, if it content her so.

Naamah.

Yet hands there be that thrid at need the harp,
Can also draw the arrow to its head
With cunning aim; and there be tongues, moreover,
That seem but moved to praise the Lord withal,
Can nevertheless shriek out the battle-cry
Madly as any.

Michal.

       I would thy jestings ceased:
Such idle parlance mated with the times
We plucked the reddened berries in the vales,
Holding one basket: Now thou dost companion
A Princess:—Nay, I meant no hurt, Naämah;
Perchance I did invite thy frowardness:

Let pass . . . Beshrew, nathless, the hap thou tellest,
That calleth the minstrel from the court away,
Leaving some stripling Benjamite to be
King's armor-bearer, when the hour is ripe
And waits the action's gathering of it . . . Not so,—
Not as the champion of the Tribes:—yet haply,
Scope had been found for some exalted deed,
Herald of such achievement as may win
Glory for Israel in the future days.
Say'st thou his father summoned? Then did he well
To go, and win the blessing of obedience.

V.

Singing Women.

1.

Praise ye the Lord most High
    With voice of psalms;
Let incense cloud the sky,
    And smoke of lambs:
Let the green earth reply
    With waving palms!

II.

Daughters of Zorah, bow
  In anguish sore:
Fair Gerar, wrap thy brow
  With sackcloth o'er:
Thy warriors, Ekron, thou
  Shalt greet no more!

III.

Low lieth thy mighty boast,
  The vultures' prey:
Thy heaven-defying host
  Our God doth slay,
And to their utmost coast
  Drive clean away.

IV.

Let cymbals clang again
  With glad accord;
—Saul hath his thousands slain;
  David's ten thousands stain
With slaughter hill and plain,—
  High sound the loud Amen;
Praise ye the Lord!

ATTENDANT.

Hearken, sweet Princess! From the casement lean,
And thou may'st catch the joyful chants of women,
The clash of tabrets and the shriek of pipes,
The acclamation,—Hear it, hear it now!
—They praise the son of Jesse, even he
That turned the battle: 'Saul hath slain his thousands,
David his tens of thousands'—

MICHAL.

Yea, enow,—
Hence, all of ye! I hear it best alone.

[*Attendants Depart.*

My heart,—my heart! That *she* should win the prize
Reckoned such evil augury, to her thought!
O, what to her the breathing melodies
At eventide? the holy Sabbath psalms?
The solemn ecstasy of Paschal-Feasts?
What those divinest pantings of a love
That breaks itself upon the strings, that so
They moan disconsolate, as with human wail?
—*She* courts oblivion of her lineage low,
And holds her state as queenly-wise as though
She were the daughter of a score of Kings.
And now,—why she will curse her lot, and chafe
To call to mind the pebbles and the sling,—

Hints of the base condition of her lord.
By gracious serviceableness that hideth power,
She will not strive to win resistless way,
Sweet of the winning, to that pathetic soul,
And deal out solace at need. . . Thou God in heaven!
Is this far world so little in Thy sight,
And mak'st Thou of Thy creatures such small account,
Thou dost regard not how all goeth awry?
—Should he as son-in-law unto the King,
Make commerce of his affluent circumstance,
And get him power, not for *his* sake,—not his,
Will be the vantage prized; but that she thus
May balsam her fretted heart. I—I, meanwhile . . .
But peace, thou puling soul! Bethink thyself,
And emulate the pride thou darest decry:
Stand up, King's daughter! At the least, be strong
Enow to hold in stately fealty
These traitorous discontents that verily
Do even imperil woman more than princess.

VI.

David.

—From mine own mouth the King thy father, learned it:
And answer made he quick, as though the thought
Had not been alien to his royal mind.
Since for thy sister, he chooseth otherwise,
Blessèd be God therefor, for evermore!
—Yet not through wanton vanity, nor to fill
All ears in Israel with my nameless name,
And so uplift upon a deed's renown
My father's house in Judah,—not to dare
Service for mine anointed King for thrall
Only of service; nor through appetence
Of an allegiance over-flusht and swollen;
Nay, nor for *thy* sake, Michal,—even for thine,
(Since I am holden to the utter truth
Nor tremble, lest it minish aught thy love,)
—For none of these, came it to pass, that I,
With arrogance unseemly in such years,
Fronted the champion who defied our hosts.
One passion swayed, unmingled, mastering, pure,
And overcame me,—fierce, consuming zeal
For the down-trodden honor of that Name
In whom all Israel trusts, that reverent Name
I speak on bended knee,—The Lord Jehovah.

—Glad,—art thou,—that no lesser motive urged?
Yea, sweet!—Who best loves Him, will best love thee.

Not all the might of this my single arm,
Not sense of right-doing, girding me within,
Not the trained uses of my field-bred craft,
Got me the victory. Even as a pebble,
Weak instrument of vengeance in His hand,
The Lord did hurl me, and the mighty foe
Fell slain thereby.
                    But, peradventure thou
Hast thoughts of other conquest in thy heart:
And crav'st to know the fashion of its on-going.
Oft sitting on the daïs, what times the King
Had me in presence that my minstrelsy
Might chase the spirit of evil from his mind,
I caught dim visions of a coiféd head
That bent and listened, behind the wind-waft screen.
So day by day I watched thy coming, still
Tracing thy tender shadow out against
The filmy hangings; side-way drooping face,
Hands held in earnest clasp, and forward reach
Of attitude attent. When I could draw
Forth strains that wrought right marvellously, I felt
It was by reason of thy presence nigh,
That made my heart leap merrily, as with wine.
And when the odorous rustle of thy garments

Told ·thou hadst passed,—the spiriting charm went too;
And on the instant all my strings waxed shrill,
As if the envious noon had drawn a-near
And stolen their delicate secret quite away.

And now . . . yea, flush, fair cheek, whereof the bloom
May shame the sunned pomegranate,—I do know,
That as a fragrant flagon kept untasted,
Thy virgin heart hath kept the wine of love
For slaking of my thirst with a refreshment
Purer, more infinite-sweet than Bethlehem's well.

THE ROYAL PREACHER.

I.

Remember thy Creator:—not when snow
  Whiter than Hermon's settleth on thy brow;
Not when thy feeble footstep tottereth slow,
That once was wont to bound as Bether's roe,
Scorning the hunter's snare,—but even now,—
  Now in thy days of youth, when memory
And mind and purpose yield as doth the stem
Of a two-summer'd palm-tree:—give to them
  The keeping of that wisdom which will be
Hard of the getting, if thou bide the hour
'Till stiffening age shall mock thy waning power,
—Before the evil days be come, or years
  Draw nigh when thou, benumbed of soul, shalt say,
"I find no pleasure in them,—naught but tears,
  For, verily, memory's self doth slip away!"

II.

While all is glad about thee,—while the sun
  Or moon or stars above be darkened not;

Before thy fainting noontide waxeth hot,
And in the east thy morn is just begun,
Remember Him who made thee. In the day
  Of lightsome youth, the clouds about the heart
  That notwithstanding gather,—quickly part,
And leave clear shining when they melt away.
But for the sad old man, the sunset ray
Is briefly kindled: Though the storm be past,
  Behind, the cleaving murk and mist remain;
  The watery gleam of promise doth not last,—
The clouds return again *after* the rain!

III.

Then all whereon thy trust was fixed, shall fail;
  The boasted keepers of thy house of clay
  Shall tremble,—the stout limbs that were thy stay,
Like strong men vanquished, bow themselves and quail
For very helplessness,—thy comforts cease
  To soothe as heretofore,—the comely grace
  Now fair to see, be wasted from thy face,—
Even to thyself betokening sure release.
The soul that through the lattice of thine eye,
  Looked forth with broadened vision, hence shall mark
A growing dimness creeping up the sky,
  And sigh by reason of the coming dark.

IV.

The doors aforetime wide-set to the throng,
   Inviting joyous entrance, then shall be
   Shut in the streets; and strange will sound to thee
The madness and the mirth that crowd along.
   The night will bring thee slumber without rest;
   And ere the earliest bird hath left its nest
To hail the day-spring, thou wilt watch for dawn,
And marvel it should crawl so slowly on,
Only to say—"Would God the hours were o'er!"
   Thy world shall sink to silence:—voices dear
   Die out to wordless murmurs in thine ear,
And music's soft delights shall charm no more.

V.

Thy heart shall vex itself with nameless fears,
   Seeing the strength that stood thy stead is gone,
   And there is left no staff to lean upon,
Along the footway of the dusking years.
White as the blossoms which the almond-tree
   Above its bald and leafless branches bears,
   Shall be the whiteness of thy thinning hairs.
The very cricket in the grass shall be
   A burden to thy flesh. Desire shall fail;
   Beauty and grace and passion, naught avail

To stir thy palsied senses. Then shall come
    The end of all,—to still the low-sunk pain:
—Neighbors shall bear thee to thy last long home,
    And through the streets shall wend the mournful train.

VI.

Or ever the mysterious silver cord
    Be loosed that to the body binds the soul,
    Or ever broken be the golden bowl
Wherein the water of our life is stored,
    Or at the fount the pitcher break that bears
Our daily draught up, or the wheel, around
Which all the mystic coils of sense are wound,
    Be stopped beside the cistern unawares,—
Then shall the dust return to earth again,
    As once it was, and mingle with its clod,—
    Then shall the spirit, set free from every chain
Wherewith the flesh had bound it,—go to God.
For this the reckoned sum of all shall be,—
That childhood, youth and age are vanity.

THE LAMENT OF JOAB.

SNATCHED from the onward rush of trampling feet,
His harness yet ungirt, and his round cheek
Pressing a dinted shield,—lay Asahel,
The boast of Judah,—Bethlehem's youngest Chief,
Of whom the deeds of valor made harvest-songs
Wherewith the reapers cheered their noontide rest.
Scarcely sufficed the mantle about him cast,
To hide the death-stab; and the bloody ooze
Was staining the trampled grass.
      Hot from pursuit,
And flushed with such a rage as yet had spared
Within his soul no silence quiet enough
For sorrow, Joab bade the host aside:
And then the Captain of an hundred fights,
Within whose bosom none made sure that even
One healthful human spot was left unseared
By scathe of war,—fell prone with grief and wail.

—"Alas, my brother! Like a netted bird
That thou should'st perish, and thy cunning spear

Trail in the dust with none avenging blow,—
          Alas, alas, my brother!

"'God's creature'—thus we named thee in our pride,
So goodly wert thou, stout of heart and limb,
So fenced about with princely gift and grace,
          Alas, alas, my brother!

"The wingéd feet that left the roe behind—
Tracked the gier-eagle home,—stretched to the goal
Ever the first,—now moveless, stony-still:
          Alas, alas, my brother!

"Behind the lattice-screen our Mother sits
Bemoaning thee, with breathless questionings thrust,
Of battle-tidings, at the passers-by:
          Alas, alas, my brother!

"We bear thee back this night across the plain
Where yesternoon thou boundedst like a stag,
And lay thee dead, for answer, at her feet:
          Alas, alas, my mother!

"Was it for this she nursed the unfathered boy
Through joyless days of desolate widowhood?
Through lone, unholpen griefs,—only for this?
          Alas, alas, my brother!

"Thy sun gone down at noon,—thy life unlived,—
Thy purpose broken off,—thy hopes plucked up,—
Thy share in youth's good heritage foregone:
   I weep, I weep, my brother!

"Now when the land is all astir through strife,
When high deeds beckon, and hot bosoms throb,—
To lay thee in the noisome sepulchre! . . .
   Ah, woe is me, my brother!"

THE WRITING OF THE KING.

A PARAPHRASE.

I said, what time my fears
Beheld the cutting asunder of my day,
—In through the gates of death I go my way,
 And leave behind the remnant of my years.

I said, I shall not see
My Lord within the land of living men,
Nor earth's inhabitants behold again,
 Nor all the mighty things that are to be.

Mine age is borne away
Even as a shepherd's tent from pasture-lands,
Or severed like the weaver's finished bands,
 Through pining sicknesses and slow decay.

I count the hours till morn
When as a lion springing in his strength
To crush his prey, Thou'lt make an end at length;
 And like a crane or swallow, I moan forlorn.

No cushat's note could be
Sadder than mine,—more filled with utter wail:
Through looking upward, lo! mine eyelids fail;
   I am oppressed; Lord, undertake for me!

'Thou shalt once more be whole:'
He surely spake!—I heard it through my tears:
'Tis He hath done it: Softly all my years
   Now shall I go in lowliness of soul.

My Lord, I live!—Thou hast
Revived my spirit: Thy recovering breath
Hath snatched me from the loathsome pit of death,
   And Thou behind Thy back my sins hast cast.

The grave, it cannot praise,
Death cannot celebrate Thy majesty;
The living, yea, the living unto Thee,
   As I this day, a thankful voice shall raise.

They shall rehearse it o'er,
Father to son,—the mercy shown the King;
And I on stringèd instruments will sing
   Within God's house His praise for evermore.

FROM GREEK STORY.

ALCYONÉ.

"Nay,—leave me not;" she cried, and her bared
    arms,
Wherefrom the saffron robe flowed back as waves
That on white Naxos break, still closer clung:

"So newly am I come within thy walls,
    That still I crave a sense of welcome nigh
To banish strangeness; and I scarce do feel
My title to thy home's sweet sovereignties,
Unless that thou be by to prove it good:
I seem no alien, when I turn to thee,
With questioning looks that read their answer writ
Large-letter'd on thy brow. But missing thee,
I sigh o'er many a precious love foregone,
Brooding upon it,—that none of all I cherished,
The tender playmates of my rock-bound Isle,
My surf-wash'd Strongylé,—do smile me back
The fond, old time, or with home-voice recall
My happy by-gone. If thou goest abroad,
I droop perforce: The past, for which thy presence
No sea-room grants, beats strong against my heart

As on our cliffs the surge was wont to beat;
And yet, how quick its ebbing, when thou dost come
To fill its hollowed depths!"

—"Thy moaning, Sweet,
Is sad as Cyprian doves' when from her isle
Their Goddess wanders. Love doth overstate
The soft self-pity of thy loneliness:
Thou knowest the violets hoard their odors best
In the night-absence of their lord, the sun:"
And Ceÿx pointed to the land-lock'd bay
Where rocked his vessel.—"Not more smooth,"—he said
"Thy molten mirror than yon crystal sea:
Confess thy fears' forecastings, little one,
Have like a goad behind thy pleadings, pricked
Keener than love even,—hurrying on thy speech,
And honeying it with artifice: Well, let
The bee snatch at the rosy lure, yet so
Escape it withal!"—and smilingly he sealed
With fast-shut kiss, the dewy-parted lips.

"But heed thou not thy pillow's scared unrest
That drones to thee of peril when I am gone:
Left now alone, keep thou my state upholden
With self-assertion of thy dignities
Of gracious wifehood,—sure that in my heart,

Thy royal realm, love busies all the hours,
Building a palace fit to be thy home.

"To Claros swiftly borne,—my doubts dissolved
Before the Oracle,—I'll haste to mount
The homeward wave; and passion, gathering strength,
And overtopping hindering circumstance,
Soon on thy bosom shall break, and ripple up
In creamy kisses, stranded on thy mouth.

"What?—eyes still cloud-wrack'd as the hidden top
Of blue Olympus? . . . Know the Immortal Gods
Claim loyal service, and I dare not put
Supreme above it, this too-sufficing love,
Lest they do frown on us with harmful brows.
Then let me go; and thou, meanwhile, high heap
Apollo's shrine: for thy on-wafting prayers
Will speed me surelier than the kindest winds
By Zephyrus loosed."

    With rapid sail full-set
Toward the far Isle, King Ceÿx from the deck
Waved light farewells to her, his weeping bride,
Who stood with outstretcht arms on the white sands,—
Even as he gazed, doting upon the tears,
The breathless throbs and palpitating doubts
Wherewith Alcyoné's so wifely love

Had wrapped itself,—as 'twere a drapery flung
In zoneless freedom above the sanctity
Of foamy swell and billowy curve, whose grace
Was heightened thereby, not hid.

      Days passed amain,
Yet brought small respite to the mind distraught
With fateful prescience and consuming dread.
The girdle that with wealth of needlecraft
Against his coming she wrought, slipt listlessly
Down from her lap, and tuneless lay the lyre
She used to touch for him,—as eve by eve,
Her vision dazed through travelling e'er so oft
The golden path he went athwart the main—
With boding heart she watched his coming.

         Thus,
Among her cushions, with her wistful face
Turned seaward, so the first white glint of sail
Might greet her sight,—ere she was 'ware, she slept,
And sleeping, dreamed. She saw above her bend
The mist-crown'd Thetis,—every look informed
With pity goddess-like; and on her ear
Fell words as sad as whispering Oreads' hid
In piney forests:

    "Thou shalt watch in vain,
O sorrowful!—shalt wait and watch in vain:

For nevermore the sail that hence hath borne
Thy darling, shall come back again to thee
Out from the purple deep, where low he lies
Couched in fair Aphrodité's coral caves."

Up-starting from her dream, Alcyoné
Uttered a cry of woe: and calling around
Her household-maidens, straightway to the beach
That stretcht afar beneath the new-risen moon,
Hasted,—her hair unbound, her milk-white feet
Unsandal'd, and her quick-caught garments flung
Girdleless to the breeze.
     Along the shore
Wailing she strayed, reaching her pleading arms
To woo him from the inexorable sea:

"O best,—O dearest!—Come to me once more!
Again,—O come again!—All life, all hope,
All cheer my soul can ever know,—all good,
I hold alone through thee: Give back thyself,
Thyself to me; I perish else,—I perish!
—Gods! Dare ye babble, ye weakling comforters,
Of other solace left? . . . As if this drear,
Wide, empty world *could* hold one joy beside,
My King being gone! Offer yon salty spray
To lips that shrivel with deadly thirst, and think

F

To quench it! O my lord,—my lord,—my life!
Better to me than all the dwellers in heaven,
Dearer to me than all the peopled earth,—
I die without thee!"

      Moaning thus she went,
Her hand-maids following, weeping at the dole
They shrank to soothe, until she reached a jut
Of headland, at whose base the waters chafed
With ceaseless lap and fret. Gazing therefrom,
Her feverish vision seized upon a blot
Of darkness on the silvery line of beach;
And turning to her followers, all dilate
With wide-eyed apprehension,—thitherward
She dumbly pointed.
     Ere their lips found words,
Fast down the ledge of splinter'd rock she sped
With delicate feet that left the wounding flints
Crimson-besprent.
     Soon as she gained the strand,
And neared the blackening speck, upon the night,
Came wafted upward to the listeners' ears,
A shriek of such unutterable bale
As held them rooted to the lichen'd shelve
With horror: for it told what not their fears
Had shaped into a thought,—that the worst woe
That could befall their mistress, had befallen,—

That whom she sought, she found,—her husband,—
    dead,
Dead,—drifted shoreward, as an ocean-weed.

They saw her rush with wringing hands to fling
Herself upon him: but betwixt the drowned
And living, swept a refluent wave that sucked
The lifeless form back to the gulfing deep,
And from the scarpéd cliff, the gazers heard
The breeze-borne words:—

   "To thee I come,—I come,
Belovéd, since thou mayst not come to me!
Reach out thine arms above the bitter brine,
And let me leap to meet thee,—thus—"

       They caught
A gleam of flickering robes,—a quick, dull plash,—
The sullen gurgle of recoiling waves,—
The clamorous screaming of a startled gull
That flapped its wings o'erhead,—but saw no more,
For all their searchings through the moonlit night,
For all their desolate wailings, nevermore
The woe-worn face of sad Alcyoné.

When wintry storms were spent, and lenient airs
Smoothed with caressing hand the furrow'd surge

Within Ægean seas,—the voyager
Watching the halcyon with his brooding mate
Nested upon the waters tranquilly
As midst Thessalian myrtles,—said,
      —" Behold
Alcyoné and Ceÿx!—We shall have
Fair weather for our sailing."

ERINNA'S SPINNING.

The Lesbian youths are all abroad to-day,
Filling the vales with mirth, and up and down
The festive streets, with roses garlanded,
Go hand in hand fair Mytilené's daughters.

Slaves follow, bearing baskets overheaped
With myrtle, ivy, lilies, hyacinths,
And all the world of sweets, wherewith to deck
The May-day altar of the flowery goddess.

And pranksome children, spilling on the paths
Acanthus-blossoms from their laden'd arms,
Come shouting after, mad with heyday glee,
Making fit ending to the gay procession.

Sweet goddess! frown not on me, though I bring
No odorous wreath to hang above thy shrine:
For, "See, Erinna!" stern my mother saith,
"Thou gaddest not abroad with idle maidens.

"The buds will all unmask without thine aid,
  The fruits round to their fullness, though no trains
  Of dallying girls thus fray the noon-time hours
  That wiser thrift should give to wheel and distaff."

And so I bide at home the day-long hours,
A prisoner at my loom: but yet my heart
Steals after my companions, while I keep
Time to their dances with my droning spindle.

I hear Alcæus strike his lyric string,
I catch our Sappho's answering choric song
On some high festival,—and my stirr'd soul
Flutters to spring beyond the bars that cage it.

O for the April birth-right of the trees!
O for the Dryad's scope to sun my thoughts
Till they unfold in myriad leafiness,
As now the quickening earth unfolds her blossoms.

But like a frost the nipping voice grates harsh:
—"Hence with thy tablets, girl! The gods above
Made thee a woman, formed for household needs,
For wifely handicraft and ministration.

"Pluck out these climbing fancies from thy thought,
  Poor, weedy things, that ape the fibrous strength

Of overshadowing man,—only to fail,
And failing so, to leave thee less a woman.

"Do what thou wilt,—gird up thy maiden-gear,—
Wrestle with athletes,—hurl the warlike dart,—
Spin forth the discus,—in the Isthmian games
Enroll thyself amid the sleek-limb'd runners;

"Or with the Delphian lyre, essay thy skill,—
Or measure dithyrambs with Æolian bards;
And for thy pains,—confess thyself outdone
Ever and always, gauged by manhood's stature."

If I make answer, that chaste Artemis
Is wise as Pythius, or the Queen of Heaven
Is strong of purpose as Olympian Jove,—
She hastes to silence me with hot impatience:

"What man of men upon a woman's face
Hath pored to learn therefrom aught other lore
Than her one lesson, love?" I answer low,
—"A woman taught her art once to a hero!"

She chafes:—"I am beholden for thy hint:
The stylus fits *thee*, sooth, as did the skein,
The hand of Hercules, who sat unsex'd
—Struck for his dulness by the queenly slipper!"

Whereat the taunt: "What youth of Lesbos, stout,
Well-knit of limb, as ripe for peace as war,
In strophes versed by seer of Chios wrought,
Will think to choose *thee* for thy trick of singing?

"Nay—talk with him of soft Milesian wools—
Of Colchian linens,—rose or saffron dyes,—
Of broidery patterns for thy silken web,—
Of Cyprian wines; the youth is fond to listen.

"'This maiden,'—(giving heed, he ponders thus,)
'Could order aptly housely offices,
Could rule discreetly the sweet realm of home,
Could rear, control and wisely guide my children.'"

Herewith she ends: "Erinna, have thou heed;
Let Lesbian virgins dance, let Sappho sing,
Improvident of wifehood's disciplines;
Thou,—rend thy scrolls, and keep thee to thy spinning."

But what care I for wifehood? . . . I, so young!
For matron dignities?—They clog and bind:
For petty talk—"*Are olives fine this year?*—"
"*Are figs full-formed?*"—Beshrew my mother's wisdom!

I would renounce them all for Sappho's bay,—
Forego them all for room to chant out free
The silent rhythms I hum within my heart,
And so for ever leave my weary spinning!

THE FLIGHT OF ARETHUSA.

I.

Near a cool Arcadian river,
   Shadowed to its broider'd brink,
By the snowy-blossom'd alders,
   Stooped a maiden down to drink.
On the hills her flying footsteps
   Had been fleet as antelope's,
While her train the Virgin-huntress
   Led along the Eléan slopes:
Till o'erweary with pursuing, she had turned aside to lave
Burning cheek and throbbing forehead in the violet-tinted wave.

II.

From her panting waist she lightly
   Let the loosen'd girdle float,
And undid the golden arrow
   That about her ivory throat

Held the purple peplon gathered,
   Till the vestment slid and fell
From her bosom's orbéd whiteness
   From her shoulder's sloping swell;
And she started from the vision which the glassing water threw,
Ravisht with the mirror'd beauty—back upon her blushing view.

III.

Buried half in ferny mosses,
   One supporting hand gleamed fair,
While its fellow freed the braidings
   Of the hyacinthine hair:
And as from the binding fillet
   Fluttered each voluptuous tress,
Leaping high, the wooing water
   Caught it in a glad caress:
When she leaned above its surface, as a crescent lily dips,
Every ripple rushed to lavish kisses on her fragrant lips.

IV.

Arms, invisibly entwining,
   Round her slender neck were thrown,
Round her neck whose veinéd opal
   Mocked the curded Thasian stone.

But the startled maiden, quivering
    Like a timorous mountain roe,
When it hears the arrow hurtle
    From Diana's silver bow,—
Snatching up her dripping ringlets from the unseen fingers' play,
Through the scented, windless thickets sprang with footed haste away.

V.

Breathlessly along the valley,
    By the tangled myrtle-glade,
Underneath the flowering citrons,
    And the aspens' flickering shade,
On she sped,—her footsteps skimming
    Fast as morning's viewless wind,
As she saw her fond pursuer
    Roll his gathering tide behind.
Then distraught she prayed for succor, and beneath her sandal'd feet
Gushed a fountain,—and her being passed into its waters sweet.

VI.

But she might not thus elude him;
    And within one pearly chain,

Sought he now to bind their currents
    That they should not part again.
When through subterranean sources,
    Soft the Naiad strove to glide,
He, by love's divining secret,
    Evermore was near her side:
Till, through long pursuit triumphant, under far Sicilia's sun,
Alpheus and Arethusa met and mingled into one.

RHODOPÉ'S SANDAL.

SLANT, arrowy beams from sheath of Helios dropt,
With golden lustre tipped the willowy marge
    Of a pellucid stream that slid
    Seaward with low, recurrent lapse,
That lulled the senses like a Lydian flute.

The lotos bowed above the tide and dreamed;
The broad-leaved calamus arose and fell
    As on a lover's breast the head
    His beating heart hath rocked to sleep;
And all the air was drowsed with tropic calm.

Parting aside the willows, coyly came
A maiden,—stealing on with furtive step
    And shy, quick-glancing eyes that turned
    Hither and thither, like a bird's,
Who fears invasion of her callow brood,

She stood and listened: There,—a heron's plash,—
O'erhead, the sunset crooning of a dove,—

The shrill cicala's cry—the purl
Of rushes laughing in their sleep—
Were all the sounds that broke the solitude.

Then, unafraid, she loosed her sandals off,
And hung her fillet on a pensile bough;
    And from her virgin waist unbound
    The crimson zone of broidery-work,
And slipt her garments from her crouching form.

Instant, she leaped, chin-deep, within the flood,
Waking the water-lilies with her plunge,
    And scattering sparkles all about,
    Until her clinging hair was crowned
With jewels bright as queenly diadem.

As thus she sported, careless and secure,
An eagle sailing from his eyried height,
    —(Her fate beneath his wings,) swooped down,
    And snatched her sandal silver-webbed,
And bore it in his beak, straight up the blue.

Across bare, yellow sands he floated high,
And poised above a royal city, saw
    A king sit on his judgment seat;
    And in his bosom dropt the prize,
As if some wingéd thing sought shelter there.

Amazed, the king from out his mantle drew
The delicate sandal,—marvelling much, if foot
　　Of zephyr or of goddess fair
　　Was fashioned in such dainty wise,
As never yet beseemed a mortal maid's.

"Now search the land!"—the monarch cried amain;
"Fly east,—fly west and south and north,—nor stay
　　Until ye find the foot that wore
　　This little sandal silver-webbed,
And lead the wearer to my palace gates."

Fast sped the messengers,—nor sped they far:
For soon they found the silver sandal's mate,
　　And fitted both upon the feet
　　That were like Psyche's, white and small,
As only formed to skim Olympian floors.

They drew the maiden from her olives' shade,
And in the simple garments that she wore,
　　Led her all-blushing, to the king,
　　Who smiling, raised her to his throne:
And thus fair Rhodopé became a queen.

THE QUENCHED BRAND.*

I.

Upon her couch the pale-cheek'd mother lay,
Her intertwining hands upraised in prayer
To Heré, for a blessing on her child,—
Her seven-days' babe, that, wrapt in leopard-skins,
    Close at her side lay sleeping.

At Calydon, King Œneus kept high feast,
And shed libations for his last-born son,
Till all the palace rang with merriment,
And the dark wine of Chios, freely drunk,
    Made glad the shouting people.

And now the revellers had parted thence,
Leaving a drowsy quiet in the halls,

---

* The only apology that can be made for handling a subject so finely and exhaustively treated in *Atalanta in Calydon*, is, that the above was written *before* the author had seen this master-piece.

That steeped Althæa's senses, as with breath
Of Attica's dew-freshened asphodels,
      Or Eastern mandragora.

At ease thus lying, with light-wingéd thoughts
Buzzing about her fruited heart like bees
About a basket-heap of amber grapes,
She smiled through inward sweet content, and reached
      To touch her boy, still smiling.

When all a-sudden, the mild-scented air
Grew murk, and chillness overhung the room,
And on the hearth the bickering flame that played
Among the cloven cedar branches, sank,—
      Swallowed in sullen ashes.

The fateful Moiræ with their stony eyes
Stood at the couch-foot: on the child they gazed,
Still softly slumbering in his dappled skins,
Then on the mother as she stretched her hands
      In awe-struck deprecation.

And Clotho spake: "Thou seest yon lighted brand;
When it hath smouldered down to leaden ash,
This sleeping child shall die: 'Tis so decreed:
Yet spare thy tears; The sight of mortals' grief
      Moves not the stern Erinyes."

Whereon they vanished. But what direst fate
May not be thwarted by a mother's love?
—Althæa trembling, weaker for her fears,
Sprang from her couch, and seizing the red brand
   Within the tall urn quenched it.

And in an ivory coffer at her side
She locked it close, ere that her maidens came;
And in her fragrant bosom dropt the key;
And all the while the little babe slept on,
   His face with smilings rippled.

II.

Fast went the years. Althæa saw her boy,
Become the pride of the Etolian land,
Wondrous for beauty,—famed for bold exploits,—
Foremost among the venturous Argonauts
   That bore the Fleece from Colchis.

And all abroad was blown his loudening praise,
When from the ravaged plains his prowess rid

The tuskéd curse, the scourge of Artemis,—
And to the warrior-sharers of the chase,
        Portioned the spoil of conquest.

Yet in the Hunt of Calydon the strife
Waxed hot, and plunging midmost in the fight,
The son of Œneus, striking right and left,
Pierced even to the death, a famous Prince,—
        His mother's nearest kinsman.

Fast-footed sped the news: "The eldest born
Of Thestius lies by Meleágros slain!"
Whereat Althæa's heart was racked with grief,—
Grief for the brother lost, and utmost rage
        Against the hand that slew him.

She tore the crescent fillet from her head,
And from her shoulders flung the queenly robe,—
And with rent locks made wail:—"Were not we twain
Nursed at one mother's bosom,—dandled each
        By the same kingly father?

"O most unhappy!—What strange madness this!
That he, my son, should smother out in blood
A mother's pity!—Hear, ye vengeful Gods!
Hear me, O Dis, Lord of the shadowy Land,
        And bid him to thy Hades!"

Thus wild she prayed, unwitting of her words:
But Atropos, the dread Unchangeable,
Heard and decreed: "The slayer shall be slain;
The fagot kept beneath the coffer's lid
      Shall quick consume to ashes."

And some stood nigh, who when the warrior came
Within the doors, made haste to utter forth
Close in his hearing, the delirious words
His sorrow-smitten mother spake when crazed
      For anguish of the fallen.

Wherefore the soul of Meleágros grew
Sullen,—defiant, and he hung aloft
His dinted armor high upon the wall,
Saying unto his wife who loosed his belt,
      —"I go no more to battle."

III.

Thereon it happed, when those who would avenge
Their Prince's death, no longer saw the Chief

Most feared of all, among the combatants,—
They laid Ætolia waste, and Calydon
        Was leaguered with their armies.

And ever as their hosts were beaten back,
Wave-like, they came again; and month by month
They battered at the walls until they shook,
And in the imminence of the close-girt siege,
        Despair stalked through the city.

"O would that Meleágros led us forth!"
The warriors sighed beneath the tottering walls;
But unavailing were their utmost pleas,
Though women came and at his threshold knelt,
        And filled his halls with wailings.

Until at length before his listless knees
The yellow-haired, fair Kleopatra fell,
And wrapped his beard about her hands and wept:
Then lightly sprang, and from the lofty wall
        Snatched down the cobwebbed helmet:

Sobbing—"My husband, put aside thy wrath;
Think on the woe that overwhelms thy land;
Think on thine ancient sire,—the hungry babes
That drain the wan-faced mothers' empty breasts,
        And wake thy soul to pity!

THE QUENCHED BRAND.

"Behold thy children!—See they seize my robe,
And cling and clamor for the bread withheld:
And this pale starveling!—Ah, the fig he craves
Is past my granting: Must we perish all,
  And thine the power to save us?"

He heard, the Leader of the mighty Hunt,
And answered not: but girt his armor on,
And strode straight outward to the yielding walls,
And gave such speech that the disheartened cried,
  —"Hope comes with Meleágros!"

He summoned whom the cruel siege had spared,
And bade the women strengthen them with food,—
Searching the cellars for last stint of wine;
And fed them to the full, while mothers wept
  At thought of starving children.

And when their hearts were cheered, he bade the gates
Fly open, and he flung the desperate band,
Himself the first, upon the unguarded foe,
And drove them far beyond Ætolia's plain,
  And back returned victorious.

No spear had scathed him, nor an arrow grazed;
And yet the harsh Erinyes, unappeased,

Forecasting his destruction, moved the men
Of Calydon to discontentful plaints
    That brake in sullen speeches.

"Behold," they said,—"this Hercules of ours!
What thanks owe we to *him?*—No love of us,
No rueing of our ills, outweighed to rend
His tame inaction: The fair-haired girl-wife
    Alone hath saved the city."

He heard their cavils, and his heart grew hot:
"Unkennel'd dogs!" he chafed,—"that snarl against
The hand that slips their chain!"—and high he hung
Upon the wall his brazen gear once more,
    Nor went among the people;

But sat within at Kleopatra's side,
And hearkened to the tales she skilled to weave
About her sire, and all the steadfast love
That won Marpessa from Apollo's grasp,—
    Marpessa, her fair mother.

And as Althæa watched his sloth, her heart
Grew envious-angry, and against her son
Turned with quick passion,—seeing his father waste,
Unhelped of him, and with her hasty breath
    She fanned the sharp vexation.

"What good doth he to Calydon,—with ears
  Full-stuffed with woolly speech, hands bounden fast
  By yonder lengths of yellow-floating hair?
  Nay! such ensample undermines the state;
       —Fates! do your work upon him!"

Then with rash hand, the blackened brand long hid
  Within the ivory coffer, forth she drew,
  And on the glowing coals of juniper
  Flung it remorseless down, and saw the flame
       With forkéd tongue enfold it.

Within his distant hall, his children nigh,
  His wife quick plying of her rattling loom,
  Himself upon some carven idless bent,—
  The face of Meleágros sudden drooped,
       Blanched with a ghastly pallor.

Spilling her shuttles on the marble floor,
  Upstarted Kleopatra with a cry
  Caught from the children rushing to sustain;
  And with her scooping hand across his brow
       She flung the lustral water.

"In vain"—he gasped—"In vain! Dark Atropos
  Draweth anear; I see her mystic form:

Come hither, little ones!—and thou, my wife,
Whom I have loved above our Calydon,
      Still let me feel thy presence.

"Thy beauty was to me beyond renown,—
Thy songs delightsomer than mouthéd praise,—
Thy love life-giving as Olympian wine;
Yea,—kiss me close!—all shall be ours again
      In the pale realm of shadows.

"Upon the flowery banks of Acheron"—
But even as he panted forth the word,
The last faint flutter on Althæa's hearth
Went out in darkness:—and the warrior lay
      Dead as the ashen embers.

BALLAD AND OTHER VERSE.

THE LADY HILDEGARDE'S WEDDING.

"I DARE not doubt his word,"—she said,
 With steadfast voice and clear;
"For sure as knight did ever plight
 True faith, he will be here.

"He sware it on this crested ring,
 That by our Lord's dear leave,
He'd wed me here at Lyndismere,
 This blessèd Christmas Eve."

—Sir Walter dallied with his blade,
 And his steel eyne grew wroth:
"Nay sweetheart, see!—it cannot be:
 Thy knight hath broke his troth."

Out spake the Lady Hildegarde
  With grieved, reproachful air:
"None other may such slander say,—
  My father only dare!

"My bower-maids all await my call,
  My bridesmen will be here;
And merry throngs with wedding songs
  Shall bide at Lyndismere."

"Now out upon thee!—simple lass!"
  With heat Sir Walter cried;
"To-morrow e'en, with seas between,
  How can'st thou be a bride?

"The Nether-land is far o'erseas,
  And angry storms may roar;
Or war may send (which Heaven forfend!)
  Tidings to vex thee sore.

"Forbear, until the galliot drop
  Anchor at Malden-head,
To fix the day, and yea or nay,
  Proclaim thou wilt be wed.

"Let the old Hall ring loud and high
  With roistering Twelfth-night cheer;

Bring holly-glow and mistletoe
   To garland Lyndismere.

"Let frolic mummers don their masks,
   Let morris-dancers come
And reel and sing in jocund ring,
   With rebeck, pipe and drum.

"Of capons, boar's-head, nut-brown ale,
   Let liberal store be shown;
And wassail-shout shall make the bout
   The merriest ever known.

"The jesters with their bells shall plot
   All mirth-provoking pranks:
So . . . let me sue;—forget Sir Hugh,
   And take thy father's thanks!"

She heard, the Lady Hildegarde,
   With firm, unflinching eye;
Then forth she stepped and onward swept,
   Disdainful of reply.

—The snows lay deep round Lyndismere,
   But generous fires blazed free,
And casements clear flashed far and near
   Their gleams across the lea.

Retainers filled the ancient Hall,
   Guests thronged as fell the night;
And rare to see, right gorgeously
   The chapel streamed with light.

"Be brave Sir Hugh come back?"—they asked
   The gray-haired seneschal:
—"'Not yet?'—'Twas said to-night he'd wed
   Our lady of the Hall."

Sir Walter chafed and strode apart;
   The cassock'd priest was seen;
And maidens fair came pair by pair . . .
   "What could the folly mean!"

A sudden vision hushed the mirth,—
   Sir Walter's breath came hard;
For last of all adown the hall
   Swept Lady Hildegarde.

"Saint Agnes!—but she's comely!" quoth
   The parti-color'd clown;
"And by the rood! in bridal hood
   And bridal veil and gown!

"Sir Hugh should e'en be here to mark
   The orange-posies bloom;

Will proxy do for stout Sir Hugh?
  Then *I* would fain be groom!"

Straight onward to the chancel rails
  The snooded maidens passed,
When suddenly the companie
  Was startled by a blast,—

A blast that echoed loud and shrill
  Without the castle-gate,
As though the train that paused amain
  Was sorely loth to wait.

Unmoved stood Lady Hildegarde,
  Nor seemed to hear nor feel,
Till up the floor, one moment more,
  There tramped a clanking heel.

"*Belovéd!*"—With one bound they met!
  Then dashing off a tear,
She turned and said with lifted head,—
  "*Father,—Sir Hugh is here!*"

FRA ANGELICO.

I.

Within Fiesolé's gray cloister-cell,
  In beatific vision wrapt apart,
  Tears on his cheek and prayer within his heart,
Kneeled a cowl'd monk. The toll of convent bell,—

II.

The iterant tread of mute Dominican
  Along the stony floor,—the soughing pines
  That sentinel'd the hills in drowsy lines,—
The gurgle of the hidden brook that ran

III.

Seaward beneath the walls,—a bleating lamb,—
  The far-off tinkle at the herds' release,—
  Were all the sounds that jarred the purple peace,
Or lightly rippled the soft-gliding calm.

IV.

Within a niche withdrawn, an easel stood
  With implements of artist-craft displayed;
  And where a missal's leaves were open laid,
Fell the slant shadow of the holy rood.

V.

Starry and golden, flame and azure hues
  Caught out of æther, waited the command
  Of that meek kneeler's mystic Master-hand,
To glorify the canvas and transfuse

VI.

The strange, seraphic beauty of his thought,
  Till the celestial impulse had sufficed
  To ray, with light divine the pictur'd Christ,
At which with awed and reverent touch he wrought.

VII.

For Art, imperious mistress, as her thrall,
  Had striven to bind him to her service fast,—
  Service, how sweet!—yet he had learned at last,
Not to forego, but consecrate it all.

VIII.

Thenceforth he sought his easel as a shrine,
  And bowed before it like an aureol'd saint

With eyes that swam the while he kneeled to paint
The marred and smitten lineaments divine.

IX.

With sunset-gold he haloed round the head
    That lay aforetime on the lowly straw,
    While visions glorious as the shepherds saw,
With sacred ecstasy his spirit fed.

X.

If from the spangled meadows any bear
    The creamy leaf the pasture-lily shows,
    Or brought him from the hedge, a folded rose,—
Some cherub's cheek their mingled tints would wear.

XI.

The mists that hallowed morning's tranquil skies,
    The crystal hoarded in the violet's cup,
    Lent their pathetic gleams to kindle up
The heaven-toucht haze of Mary's clouded eyes.

XII.

And thus he served the Master, while he trod
    The path he loved the best,—inspired to fill
    His work with worship's rapture, climbing still
Beauty's ascending steps that lead to God.

XIII.

"*Beáto:*"—So they named him: and by this,
Down-drifting to us from the Long Ago,
The pure, enthusiast life we come to know,
That gave to Art its holiest types of bliss.

THE NAMELESS PILGRIM.*

"Now where-away fare ye, son of mine?"—
    Ædwen the mother said;
"And why are these stalwart limbs of thine
    So weary and ill-bestead?"

—"A-weary am I, with woeful ruth,
    Thou sayest it, mother sweet;
For he that I served with a liegeman's truth,
    Hath trodden me underfeet."

"Now who be the baron foul or fair,
    Saxon or Norman he,
Requiteth thy fealty thus?—declare
    Wherefore he chode with thee."

And Godric made answer:—"Sooth to tell,
    'Tis a tale thou hast heard afore:
The World is the Master I wrought for well,
    But he payeth me wage no more.

---
* An incident in the life of the Saxon hermit, Saint Godric.

"With a gnawing hunger I craved the bread
    I had eaten through riotous years;
My trencher he heaped with ashes instead,
    And for wine he poured me tears."

Then Ædwen the mother was tearful-glad,
    And she claspt her agéd palms,
And lifted to heaven her eyes, long sad,
    And worshipped the Lord in psalms.

"Naught other vassalage wilt thou seek?"
    She questioned in hope and fear;
—"I would have thee fain of the fen-lands speak,
    And thy home on the marshy Wear."

"Nay, never again by the marshy Wear
    Will I fashion my wattled home;
For a pilgrim,—ye wot by the token here,—
    Now wendeth his way to Rome."

"O blesséd Saint Cuthbert of The Isles!"
    Cried Ædwen,—"In very deed,
Thou hast heard my prayers, and hast rent the wiles,
    And the thrall of sin is freed!

"I also a pilgrim's pains would feel,—
    Thirst, weariness, hunger, heat;

I also, for Christ's sweet sake, would kneel
  At the Holy Father's feet."

Then Ædwen and Godric, hand in hand
  Journeyed o'er broomy down,
Across gray moor and pasture-land,
  By thorpe and stead and town:

And as they neared the shingly beach,
  Adown by the billows blue,
A maiden drew nigh, and with silvery speech
  Said,—"I am a pilgrim too."

The fierce, stout gaze of Godric quailed
  As he met her dove-like look,
And his spirit, in pride of manhood mailed,
  Like a reed of the river shook.

They spared to question her of her name,
  Of her high or low degree;
But trusting and trusted, on they came
  To the shore of the surging sea.

Through the vineyard paths they winned their way,
  And the hours of travail o'er,
They laid them down at the set of day
  On many a threshing-floor.

And Ædwen the mother her mantle spread
    And covered the maiden sweet,
As she rested her innocent, down-dropt head
    On the piles of the golden wheat.

By the wayside cross and the forest shrine,
    As they knelt at their noontide prayer,
The sunbeams seemed in a haste to twine
    A circle about her hair.

Onward they toiled through windy pines,
    By torrents a-flash with foam,
And compassed the crested Apennines,
    And gazed on the walls of Rome.

With daily penance and prayer and psalm,
    Each hallowéd aisle they trod,
Till the restless bosom had won the calm
    Of a spirit at peace with God.

And ever and aye, the twain between,
    With a pure, uplifted face,
The blue-eyed maiden walked serene,
    In her saintly, slender grace.

Their vows performed and their alms-deeds done,
    Homeward their way they bent,

And close beside, like a wimpled nun,
    The beautiful stranger went.

And back o'er the billowy Apennines,
    By meadow and garth and lea,
Through orchards of olives and purpling vines,
    They came to the surging sea.

And then, with a wave of her filmy hands,
    As they touched the farther shore,
The maiden glided athwart the sands,
    And they saw her face no more.

—"Now what is thy thought, O mother mine?"
    Cried Godric marvelling thus;
"Whence came,—whither went the form divine
    That hath journeyed so long with us?"

Said Ædwen,—"The whither she goeth I ween
    No more I wete than ye;
But certes,—Saint Catherine's self hath been
    One of the pilgrims three!"

THE DUMB POET.

I.

HE does not wind about his thought
    Iambics flexile as the willow;
His surge of feeling is not wrought
    Into a foamy line of billow.

II.

His garden of Hesperides
    Displays no trim-set, bounded border,
And o'er it his Hymettian bees
    Hum in mellifluous disorder.

III.

In rhythmic, art-constructed cells
    He does not hive the Attic honey
He finds deep hid in darksome dells,
    Or stored in clover-pastures sunny.

IV.

From evening's streaks of threaded light
    That woof the sky with hues elysian,

He is not skilled to weave aright
　　The iris of the poet's vision.

V.

The brook, soft lapsing o'er the sand
　　In bubbling laughters,—shallow'd slumbers,
He does not pour with gauging hand
　　Into the jewel'd cup of numbers.

VI.

He cannot strain the robin's brief,
　　One-thoughted song into a sonnet;
Nor catch the wavering maple-leaf,
　　To trace an autumn pastoral on it.

VII.

Yet never to the poet's view
　　Did liberal Nature e'er discover
More of the secrets sweet and true
　　She tells to none but those who love her.

VIII.

The break of morning holds for him
　　A joy beyond all words' revealing;
And pictures, vast, mysterious, dim,
　　Illumine twilight's frescoed ceiling.

IX.

Like litanies, the murmurous rain
  Makes a cathedral-service solemn;
He hears the myriad-voiced "*Amen*"
  Beneath each leafy arch and column.

X.

The wheat that bows its ripen'd head,
  The meadow steeped in purple glory,
The landscape-page before him spread,—
  Are cantos of his Epic Story!

XI.

From Nature,—true Permessian source,
  Wells the pure joy of feeling,—seeing;
But Love inspires the lyric force
  That shapes the Idyl of his being.

XII.

The golden missal of the Past,
  With rich illuminations burning,
Love blazoned it from first to last,—
  And see! . . . its leaves are worn with turning!

XIII.

He *lives* his Poem:—day by day,
  Its choric chime his thought engages:

And songs of hope are stored away
  Within the future's uncut pages.

XIV.

O my Dumb Poet, in whose soul
  Love still the mystic psalm rehearses,
Make thou mine open heart thy scroll,
  And fill it with thy marvellous verses!

THE BABY'S MESSAGE.

I.

"O, IT is beautiful!—Lifted so high,—
Up where the stars are,—into the sky,—
Out of the fierce, dark grasp of pain,
Into the rapturous light again!

II.

"Whence do ye bear me, shining ones,
Over the dazzling paths of suns?
Wherefore am I thus caught away
Out of my mother's arms to-day?

III.

"Never before have I left her breast,—
Never been elsewhere rocked to rest:
Yet,—I am wrapt in a maze of bliss,
Tell me what the mystery is!"

IV.

—"Baby-spirit, whose wondering eyes
Kindle, ecstatic with surprise,

This is the ending of earthly breath,—
This is what mortals mean by death.

V.

"Far in the silences of the blue,
See where the splendor pulses through;
Thither, released from a world of sin,
Thither we come to guide thee in:

VI.

"In through each seven-fold, circling band,—
In where the white child-angels stand,—
Up to the throne, that thou mayest see
Him who was once a babe like thee."

VII.

—"O ye seraphs of love and light!
Stay for a little your lofty flight:
Stay, and adown the star-sown track,
Haste to my weeper,—haste ye back!

VIII.

"Tell her how filled and thrilled I am,—
Tell her how wrapt in boundless calm:
Tell her I soar, I sing, I shine,—
Tell her the heaven of heavens is mine!"

IX.

—"Tenderest comforter,—Faith's own word,
Sweeter than ours, her heart hath heard:
Softly her solac'd tears now fall;
Christ's one whisper hath told her all!"

ATTAINMENT.

[CARMEN NATALE.]

I.

RARE-RIPE, with rich, concentrate sweetness,
    All girlish crudities subdued,
You stand to-day, in the completeness
    Of your consummate womanhood.

II.

The stem supports no useless flower,
    No simply graceful spathic shoot;
But all, through fostering sun and shower,
    Develops into perfect fruit.

III.

And this is what we looked for:—Can it
    Fail of such ends in Nature's law?
—Who marvels at the full pomegranate,
    That watched the blossom pure from flaw?

IV.

Yet something more than summer weather
  Ambers the heavy-cluster'd vine;
Fierce heats,—slant rains combine together
  To fill the bounteous grapes with wine.

V.

We heed too carelessly the uses
  Of the rude buffets of the wind,
That vivify the quicken'd juices,
  And crimson-tint the fruity rind.

VI.

But while we mark the mellow'd grace,
  Whose cultur'd sweetness never cloys,—
We yet have found that sorrow's traces
  Are in the down-bloom, more than joy's.

VII.

We learn through trial: 'Tis the story
  World-old and weary; and we know,
Though we disclaim the wisdom hoary,
  That all our tests will prove it so.

VIII.

You've conned the lesson: every feature
  Is instinct with the dear-bought lore:

You comprehend how far the creature
    Can meet the creature's need:—And more

IX.

Than this; you've gauged and weighed the human,
    With just, deliberate, fixt control,
And found the perfect poise of woman,—
    The pivot-balance of her soul!

X.

And thus,—sustained and strengthened by it,—
    You front the future: Bring it balm
Or bring it bitter,—no disquiet
    Shall mar the inviolable calm.

XI.

Let the years come! They shall but double
    God's benison within your breast;
Nor time, nor care, nor change shall trouble
    The halcyon of this central rest.

THE SIGNAL.

"Draw rein there!—your horses are tramping
    An orange-boy under their feet!"
But onward, their silver bits champing,
    They swept through the roar of the street.

Wrapped softly in cashmere and laces,
    In her phaeton a lady rolled fast,
Nor paused to know wherefore the faces
    That turned on her, paled as she passed.

When the surges are parted that hide him,
    They see on the pitiless stones
A child with his basket beside him,
    Too wounded for shrieking or groans.

Kind arms are stretched forward to shield him,
    —Thank God that such always we see!
And the help that they hasten to yield him
    Is as tender as woman's would be.

—In the ward of a hospital lying,
  Where never a glimmer of joy
Played over the sick and the dying,
  The life-light came back to the boy.

No soldier in front of the battle,
  Struck down where the terrible rain
Of shot filled his ear with its rattle,
  Bore braver his burden of pain.

Yet how could they tell, or he ask it,
  Nor melt with regret or alarm?
The arm that had carried his basket,—
  He must lose it,—that little right arm!

One night when the dread of it vexed him,
  The quietest sobbings were heard;
And a child in the couch that was next him,
  Whose innermost pity was stirred,—

Broke softly the silence so stilly,
  And lifting his finger, said—"Hark!
There's somebody crying!—O, Willie,
  Now why do you sob in the dark?

"I know what must happen to-morrow;
  But haven't you heard how the Lord

Takes pity on us in our sorrow,
    As He walks through the hospital ward?

"So ask Him to help you whenever
    His beautiful face is in sight;
He'll not overlook you,—O, never!
    Perhaps He is coming to-night."

A gleam of the suddenest gladness
    Across the wet eye-lashes stole;
And he answered,—and smiled down the sadness
    That just had been clouding his soul,—

"I've heard when the children grow weary—
    For how can their hearts understand?
—That they feel through the darkness so dreary,
    As He passes, and catch at His hand.

"And He leads them away to that far light,
    Where never comes sickness or woe,
Right up through the path of the starlight,—
    I think I will ask Him to go.

"And lest I should fail to be keeping
    Strict watch,—for I'm tired and weak,
And Jesus might pass while I'm sleeping,
    Nor know that I wanted to speak;—

"Like a signal they raise o'er the billows,
    When sailors are shipwrecked,—I'll prop
My arm that is broken, with pillows,
    And then He will see it,—and stop.

"And I'll hear through the midnight so chilly,
    His voice whisper, gently and low,
'Are you waiting to go with me, Willie?'
    And I'll answer,—'I'm waiting to go.'"

—When the light of the morning had broken,
    And the bells with a chiming accord
Were pealing their earliest token
    Like a hymn through the hospital ward,—

They saw,—and the marvel grew deeper,
    The pillow-propt arm was so wan:
They uncovered the face of the sleeper,
    And wondered to find,—he was gone!

UNVISITED.

Her heart was like a spring,—this gentle friend's,
With ceaseless flow of heavenliest charities,—
A spring upon whose brink the anemonés
And hooded violets and shrinking ferns
And tremulous woodland things crowd unafraid,
Sure of the freshening that they always find.

Her smile was prodigal of summery shine,—
Gayly persistent,—like a morn in June
That laughs away the clouds, and up and down
Goes making merry with the ripening grain,
That slowly ripples,—its bent head drooped down,
With golden secret of the sheathéd seed;—
A mischievous morn, that smites the poppies' cheeks
Among the corn, till they are crimsoning
With bashful flutterings,—a right prankish morn
That with a frolic flow of mirthfulness,
Kisses the bramble-blossoms till they blush.

Yet she who loved all beauty, seeing therein
The human, the divine,—faint lineaments,
Suggestions instinct with the All-Beautiful,
Silently slipt away, and left the flowers
Athirst, through missing of the moisten'd cool.

Most meet it surely were for such as she,
To take her quietest sleep where all of fair,
And all of gladdest things should crowd around
To soothe and broider o'er the covering sod;
Where story-telling brook,—responsive leaves,
The mossy epigraph and carvings quaint
Of cypress aisles,—the solemn organ-dirge
Of the full-throated wind,—the pipe and coo
Of thrushes,—Nature's purest choristers,—
Might mingle with the flow of children's voices,
As through their tears they smiled to read her name,
And sobbing for pity, kissed it, on the stone.
No otherwhere should heart so genial rest
Than near the tombs of kindred best-beloved,
Who hand-in-hand with her, had trod life's path,—
Letting go, only at death's low lich-gate,
To clasp, the other side. And yet this heart,
So toucht with softest yearnings, moulders now
Where not one passion-flower of love sends up
The frailest tendril,—where no little feet
Wear a pathetic footway round her grave

With daily treadings—where pale memory
Can never bear her golden reliquary,
To gather the dropt blooms and hoard them close,
Heightening their odors with the balm of tears.

AN ALPINE PICTURE.

[AFTER RUSKIN.]

Ferny pastures, beetling rock,
  Slopes half-islanded by streams,
  Glisten in the amber gleams
Of the sunshine,—gleams that mock
Shadow'd field and cool grey rock.

Farther up, the sobbing pines
  Hold their uncontested sway,
  Shutting out the smiling day
With their sullen, serried lines,
—Mournful, melancholy pines!

Through them, with eternal roar,
  From the glaciers, thunder deep
  Cataracts, whose tremendous leap
Pales them, plunging evermore
Shuddering through the twilight roar:

AN ALPINE PICTURE.

Filling with their misty cold,
   All the gorges in their fall,
   As athwart the granite wall
Which they loosen from its hold,
Down they shiver, blanched with cold.

Thread this craggy mountain-path
   Fringed with ferns that shun the light;
   Climb the ridg'd and rugged height:
Stand within the arch that hath
Bounded in the curving path.

Dark against the whitened foam,
   Rises a rude cross of pine,
   Whose mysterious, sacred sign
Lifts the thoughts that guideless roam,
Skyward, through the eddying foam.

From the lichen'd foothold gaze
   Out upon the pale, far sky,
   Where the peaks that stretch so high
Catch the roseate, dying day's
Faint-shot flushes, as you gaze.

Drop your vision fathoms down
   Yonder cavernous abyss,
   Where the torrents seethe and hiss,

And the jaggéd snow-crags frown,
Drop it like a plummet down.

Sheer along the laboring steep,
   Where the traveller's alpenstock
   Needs must pierce the crevic'd rock,
Let your straining glances sweep,
Measuring all the toilsome steep.

Then, look up!—See how the cross
   Casts its symbol-shade sublime
   O'er the wrack and roar of time,—
O'er its fret and moil and loss:
So! . . . we'll rest here,—at the cross.

THE COLOR-BEARER.

The shock of battle swept the lines,
   And wounded men and slain
Lay thick as lie in summer fields
   The ridgy swathes of grain.

The deadly phalanx belched its fire,
   The raking cannon pealed,
The lightning-flash of bayonets
   Went glittering round the field.

On rushed the steady *Twenty-Fourth*
   Against the bristling guns,
As if *their* gleams could daunt no more
   Than that October sun's.

It mattered not though heads went down,
   Though gallant steps were stayed,
Though rifles dropped from bleeding hands,
   And ghastly gaps were made,—

"*Close up!*"—was still the stern command,
  And with unwavering tread,
They held right on, though well they knew
  They tracked their way with dead.

As fast they pressed with laboring breath,
  Clinched teeth and knitted frown,
The sharp, arrestive cry rang out,—
  "*The color-bearer's down!*"

Quick to the front sprang, at the word,
  The youngest of the band,
And caught the flag still tightly held
  Within the fallen hand.

With cheer he reared it high again,
  Yet claimed one instant's pause
To lift the dying head and see
  What comrade's face it was.

"*Forward!*"—the captain shouted loud,
  Still "*Forward!*"—and the men
Snatched madly up the shrill command,
  And shrieked it out again.

But like a statue stood the boy,
  Without a foot's advance,

Until the captain shook his arm,
    And roused him from his trance.

—His home had flashed upon his sight,
    The peaceful, sunny spot!
He did not hear the crashing shells,
    Nor heed the hissing shot.

He saw his mother wring her hands,
    He caught his sister's shriek,—
And sudden anguish racked his brow,
    And blanched his ruddy cheek.

The touch dissolved the spell,—he knew,
    He felt the fearful stir;
He raised his head and softly said,
    —"He was my brother, sir!"

Then grasping firm the crimson flag
    He flung it free and high,
While patriot-passion stanched his grief,
    And drank its channels dry.

Between his close-set teeth he spake,
    And hard he drew his breath,—
"God help me, sir,—I'll bear this flag
    To victory,—or to death!"

The bellowing batteries thundered on,
    The sulph'rous smoke rose higher,
And from the columns in their front,
    Poured forth the galling fire.

But where the bullets thickest fell,
    Where hottest raged the fight,
The steady colors tossed aloft
    Their blood-red trail of light.

Firm and indomitable still
    The *Twenty-Fourth* moved on,
A dauntless remnant only left,—
    The staunch three-score were gone!

And now once more the shout arose
    Which not the guns could drown,—
"Ho, boys!—Up with the flag again!
    The color-bearer's down!"

They strove to free his grasp,—but fast
    He clung with desperate will;
—"The arm that's broken is my *left*,
    See!—I can hold it still!"

And "*Forward! Twenty-Fourth!*" rang out
    Above the deafening roar,

Till, all at once, the colors lowered,
   Sank, and were seen no more.

And when the stubborn fight was done,
   And from the fast-held field
The order'd remnant slow retired,
   Too resolute to yield,—

They found a boy whose face still wore
   A look resolved and grand,
Who held a riddled flag close clutched
   Within his shatter'd hand.

NINETEEN.

I.

My maiden of the violet eyes,
  White-lidded as the mists of morning,
Half clouded with a coy surprise
  Their changeful, shimmering depths adorning:—

II.

Fresh-lipped like any night-shut rose,
  Beaded with youth's delicious potion,—
And cheeks whose colour comes and goes
  As comes and goes the quick emotion:

III.

The vernal flush of fresh nineteen,
  With all its clear, auroral glory,
Enrobes you like a fairy queen
  Within a realm of fairy story.

IV.

You breathe so rarefied an air,
  No rainy films, no hazes seeing,

Our sluggish pulses could not bear
  The atmosphere that feeds your being.

V.

So golden seems the lustrous reach
  Of the long summer day before you,—
So boundless the aërial stretch
  Of the blue heavens' enchantment o'er you,—

VI.

You cannot know nor understand
  How those pale hills so softly distant
Can steep the broad, sunshiny land
  In shadows gradual, sure, persistent.

VII.

You comprehend that life has care;
  You've seen it oft grow grand with duty;
Through small attritions watched it wear,
  Till shorn of all its earlier beauty:

VIII.

And you have said—"It shall not be
  Thus with *my* morning's pearly promise;
We *need* not,—if we *will* not,—see
  The beautiful go drifting from us."

IX.

My maiden of the violet eyes,
   Forget in faith so pure and holy,
That gloom upon the mountain lies,—
   Dusk in the gorges darkens slowly.

X.

Descend not from your æther-height
   To meet the shadows: Let them rather
Wind low along the vales where night
   Begins her hooded mists to gather.

XI.

Keep on your lips the fragrant dew,
   And in your eyes the sheen so tender;
Youth's morning dawns but once, and you
   But once can walk its rubied splendor!

WINE ON THE LEES.

"TWELVE years ago to-day:—how short it seems!
And but that you have calendared the time
Beyond disproof, I should affirm it less
By half a dozen, since that English June
Gave me the English Margaret for my wife.
Do you remember how we wrangled, strove,
Grew angry and made up a score of times,
Ere we made sure the memorable day—
The golden pivot upon which should turn
Our circling future?"

                "Ah,—so like a man,
To question my remembrance! Woman's heart
Is not the waxen tablet that you feign;
Love's stylus wears, for her, a diamond point,
And smoothe the plastic surface as she may,
It cuts into the ivory beneath,
And leaves its sharp, incisive characters
Graven there for ever. Wiser man, you see,
Gives love a reed to write with: there's the difference."

"My inconclusive, sweet philosopher!
Was it a reed I wrote with, when I scored
Down in my scroll of life, that Tenth of June?"

"Nay,—for the nonce, I lent my diamond point:
Or rather, I insist it *was* a reed,
But that the tablet being a woman's heart,
Love's lightest mark became indelible.
—Once groove your name upon a sapling's rind,
And all the erasing years of storm and shine
Will only greaten it, until the scar
Becomes exaggerate in its knotted bole:
And even so . . ."

                "I do accept it, Sweet!
But memory cannot hold a mirror up
Clearer to you, reflecting fairly back
The precious nothings of that bridal-morn
Than now to me. How well I can recall,
Each sense seemed doubly keen: how full I heard
A lark's song, dropping from a loftier height
Than ever before; and even the overmuch
Oppressive hawthorn-scents,—and how I saw
The bridal-favors at your horses' ears
A long half mile off—"

                "If it comes to that,
I knew the moment when your eye first caught

Sight of our carriages; you stopped to take
The hedge-rose offered by the cottage-girl—"

"Yes!—with the 'fair good morrow,' that I thought
So fortunate an omen—"

"That you gave
It me before our greeting,—I remember!
I have it yet, prest 'twixt our wedding-cards,
To show to Madge, when she is old enough:—"

"And I,—you know the box of sandal-wood
That holds my dear dead mother's tress of hair,
And other precious things:—this golden key
Here on my chain unlocks it;—Well, beneath
Those packages of lavender'd letters, tied
With ribbon fresh a dozen years ago,
I hide with jealous care, a torn, white glove.
Do you forget, that as we stood together
One moment in the porch of Thorncliffe Church,
Just ere we walked the aisle,—you strove to draw
Your glove with tremulous fingers on your hand,
And rent it piteously? A pretty passion
It was to watch!"

"O, ay,—I see it all!
You, looking down in your seigneurial calm,

On the close-hooded falcon at your wrist,
For whom the jess was fastening!"

    —"Mock on so!
I love to feel the flutter of your wings
Under my hand, full conscious all the while,
That did I spread it wide and bid you fly,
I could not shake you from your chosen perch.
Yet say,—the truth bears thousand repetitions,—
Say that you would not, were the power vouchsafed,
Stand in your still unclaimed and girlish grace
Free, in the porch of Thorncliffe Church again."

"So would not I:—For me these years have wrought
To their full round all woman's experiences,—
Wifehood most blesséd,—precious motherhood:
And so with leave to choose, I would not be,
From queen to peasant, aught else than what I am.
And yet the gift of gifts is youth: I scarce
Was twenty then—"
    "And twenty cannot be
Full-sunned, heart-savour'd, mellow as thirty-two.
For youth's acerbities can set the teeth
At times on edge,—its alternating airs
Of gust and calm, most easy to be borne
By lovers in patient faith, may yet become
Siroccos unto husbands;—its weak gauge

Of life and life's significant loveliness,
Be reconcilement for the easy loss
Of tendril-graces that climb about the heart,
And smother it with over-flush of bloom.
Give me then, summer with the sheen of spring,—
The tropic fruit, inclusive of the flower,—
Noon with the dew still on it,—progressive years,
With childhood's zest,—an 't please you, thirty-two!

"But see,—the veil of woven gold pales off
The sunset hills; and now before our Madge
Comes clamoring for her nightly cradle-song,
Or Harry with his tangled paradigms
Beseeches furtherance with *amo,—amare,—*
Let loose your fingers on the ivory keys,
And sing the snatch I scribbled you yesterday."

"Fill the jewel-crusted beaker
   From the earliest vine;
Gather grapes, ambrosia-fruited,
   And express their wine:

"Honey'd, lucent, amber-tinted;
   —Could old Massic shine
With a foam whose beaded opals
   Sunnier globes enshrine?

"When did ivy-crown'd Bacchanté
    Warmer clusters twine
Round a Ganymedian chalice?
    Yet these lips of mine

"Sometimes crave a racier vintage,—
    Sometimes dare to pine
For that wondrous, witching essence,
    Orient muscadine,—

"Balmed with immemorial richness,
    Like a royal line,—
Such as slumbrous decades ripen
    Through their long decline.

"Hence then, young love's pearl-rimm'd flagon
    Keep the pale-flusht wine;
Earth it, till its juices fruiten—
    Till the lees refine;—

"Till each tinge of harshness mellows,—
    Till all sweets combine
To prepare a draught quintessent,
    Rapturous, pure, divine!"

A YEAR IN HEAVEN.

I.

A YEAR uncalendar'd ;—for what
    Hast thou to do with mortal time?
Its dole of moments entereth not
    That circle, infinite, sublime,
Whose unreached centre is the throne
    Of Him before whose awful brow
Meeting eternities are known
    As but an everlasting *Now!*
The thought uplifts thee far away,—
    Too far beyond my love and tears;
Ah, let me hold thee as I may,
    And count thy time by earthly years.

II.

A year of blessedness, wherein
    No faintest cloud hath crost thy soul;
No throe of pain, no taint of sin,
    No frail mortality's control:

Nor once hath disappointment stung,
   Nor care, world-weary, made thee pine;
But rapture such as human tongue
   Hath found no language for, is thine.
Made perfect at thy passing,—who
   Dare sum thine added glory now,
As onward, upward,—pressing through
   The ranks that with veiled faces bow,—
Ascending still from height to height,
   Fearless where, hush'd, the seraphs trod,
Unfaltering midst the circles bright,
   Thou tendest inward unto God?

III.

A year of progress in the lore
   That is not learned on earth: Thy mind,
Unclogged of clay, and free to soar,
   Hath left the realms of doubt behind.
And mysteries which thy finite thought
   In vain essayed to solve, appear
To thine untasked inquiries fraught
   With explanation strangely clear.
Thy reason owns no forced control
   As held it here in needful thrall,
God's secrets court thy questioning soul,
   And thou may'st search and know them all.

IV.

A year of love;—Thy yearning heart
  Was always tender even to tears,
And sympathy's responsive art
  Lent its warm coloring to thy years:
But love whose wordless ecstasy
  Had overborne the finite,—now
Throbs through thy saintly purity,
  And burns upon thy dazzling brow.
For thou the hands' dear clasp hast felt
  That show the nail-prints still displayed,
And thou before the face hast knelt
  That wears the scars the thorns have made.

.V.

A year without thee:—I had thought
  My orphan'd heart would break and die,
Ere time had meek quiescence wrought,
  Or soothed the tears it could not dry.
And yet I live,—to faint, to groan,
  To stagger with the woe I bear,
To miss thee so!—to moan and moan
  The name I dare not breathe in prayer!
Thou praising,—while I weakly pine,—
  Enraptured,—while I sorrow sore,—
And thus betwixt thy soul and mine
  The distance widening evermore!

VI.

A year of tears to me;—to thee,
  The end of thy probation's strife,
The archway to eternity,
  The portal of thy deathless life:
To me,—the corse, the bier, the sod,—
  To thee,—the palm of victory given:
Enough, my bruiséd heart!—Thank God
  That thou *hast* been a year in heaven!

AFTERNOON.

I.

You say the years have sadder grown
　Beneath their weight of care and duty,—
That all the festive grace has flown
　That garlanded their earlier beauty.

II.

You tell me Hope no more can daze
　Your vision with her bland delusions;
Nor Fancy, versed in subtle ways,
　Seduce you to her gay conclusions.

III.

The rapturous throb,—the bound,—the flush,
　That made all life one strong sensation,
Grow quiet now beneath the hush
　Of time's profounder revelation.

IV.

You have it still, the inviolate past,
   So pure from all illusive glitter,—
So luminous-clear from first to last,
   With scarce the needful dash of bitter.

V.

Vixi:—Thus, looking back, you write;
   The best that life can give, you've tasted;
And drop by drop, translucent, bright,
   You've sipped and drained;—not one is wasted.

VI.

Yet not in retrospect your eye
   Alone sees pathways pied with flowers;
You knew, the while the hours flew by,
   They were supremely blissful hours.

VII.

The sun slopes slowly westering still,
   Behind you now your shadow lengthens,
And in the vale beneath the hill
   The evening's growing purple strengthens.

VIII.

The morning mists that swam your eye,
   Too vaguely wrapped your young ideal:

Now,—cut against your clearer sky,
  You comprehend the true—the real.

IX.

Life still has joys that do not pall,
  Love still has hours serene and tender:
'Tis afternoon, dear! . . . that is all!
  And this is afternoon's calm splendor.

X.

God grant your cloudless orb may run
  Long, golden cycles ere we sever;
Or, like the northern midnight-sun,
  Circle with light my heart for ever!

POOR CARLOTTA.

The scion of immemorial lines,
   August with histories hoary,
Whose grand, imperial heirship shines
   With the starriest names of story,—
Stands doomed to die:—and the grenadiers
   In serried and silent column,
Their pitiless eyes half-hazed with tears,
   Are waiting the signal solemn.

The brave young Emperor lifts his brow,—
   It never has shown so regal;
Yet it is not the pride of the Hapsburg now,
   Nor the glance of the clefted eagle.
No blazing coronet binds his head,
   No ermined purple is round him;
But his manhood's majesty instead
   With royaller rank has crowned him.

An instant's space he is caught away
   To Schönbrunn's peaceful bowers;

There's a lightning-dazzle of boyhood's day,
  —Vienna's glittering towers
Flash back with a mocking, blinding glare;
  —To barter such princely splendor,
For wrecked ambition and stark despair,—
  Betrayal and base surrender!

Wild, infinite, taunting memories thrill
  His soul to its molten centre;
Remorses that madden him, clamor still,
  But he will not let them enter.
The grovelling traffic of time all done,
  He would have the temple lonely . . .
Its sanctuaries emptied one by one,
  That God may fill it only.

But under the Austrian skies afar,
  Aglow with a light elysian,
The mullion'd windows of Miramar
  Loom out on his tortured vision:
He looks on its grey abeles again;
  He is threading its pleachéd alleys;
He is guiding his darling's slacken'd rein,
  As they scour the dimpled valleys.

. . . He can gaze his last on the earth and sky,—
  Step forth to his doom, nor shiver,—

Eternity front his steadfast eye,
  And never a muscle quiver:
But love's heart-rackings, despairs and tears
  Wrench the fixt lips asunder;
— '*My poor Carlotta!*'—Now, grenadiers,
  Your volley may belch its thunder!

THE COMPLAINT OF SANTA CLAUS.

The snow lies deep on the frozen ground,
    And the Christmas-night is cold,
And I shiver before the rime so hoar,—
    Can it be I am growing old?

Long years agone, when the Christmas chimes
    Made merry the midnight sky;
When the carollers' call filled house and hall,
    And wassail and mirth ran high;—

When harlequin mummers reveled and danced,
    And the great Yule-log blazed bright;—
And the walls were green with a summer sheen,
    In holly and yew bedight;—

When the faces of all, the young, the old,
    Were brimming with sparkling cheer,—
Ay, those were the times when Christmas chimes
    Were the merriest sounds of the year!

I snapped my fingers in Jack Frost's teeth,
   While the snow was wavering down,
And the icicles flung from my beard that hung,
   —My beard that was then so brown,—

And I wrapped myself in my grizzly coat,
   And lit my pipe with a coal
From Hecla's crest, where I stopped to rest
   On my way from the Northern Pole.

My reindeers—O they were brisk and gay!
   My sledge, it could stand a pull;
My pack though great, seemed a feather's weight,
   No matter how crammed and full.

My heart, it was stout in those good old days,
   And warm with an inward glee;
For I thought of the mirths of a thousand hearths,
   Where the little ones watched for me.

So I gathered my sweets from far and near,
   And I piled my cunningest toys,
(Unheeding the swirls) for the innocent girls,
   And the rollicking, roguish boys.

But the times have sobered and changed since then,
   My merriment flags forlorn; .

THE COMPLAINT OF SANTA CLAUS.

My beard is as white as on Christmas-night
    Of old was the Glaston thorn.

Though my wither'd lips still hold the pipe,
    No longer the smoke-wreath curls;
But saddest to see of sights for me,
    —My frolicsome boys and girls

Have grown so knowing they dare to say—
    These Protestants wise and small,—
That all saints deceive, and they don't believe
    In a *Santa Claus* at all!

Ah me! 'Tis a fateful sound to hear;
    'Tis gall in my wassail-cup:
The darlings I've spoiled, so wrought-for and toiled,
    The children have given me up!

My heart is broken;—I'll break my pipe,
    And my tinkling team may go,
And bury my sledge on the trackless edge
    Of a Lapland waste of snow.

My useless pack I will fling away,
    And in Germany's forests hoar,
From the icy steep I will plunge leagues deep,
    And never be heard of more.

UNREASON.

I.

When the far port is neared at last,
   And underneath the storm-tost feet
   That trod the deck through Tropics' heat,
And Norland winter's iciest blast,
The firm, sure earth is anchored fast,—
   We give the voyager "All hail!"
   Thou,—anchored safe within the veil,
Chide not, because athwart the foam
That beats betwixt me and thy home,
   Weeping to miss thy vanished sail,
   I find no voice to cry—"All hail!"

II.

Shall he who wrought with tireless hands,
   That only slackened when the seed,
   Sown with such self-contemning heed,
Seemed but to parch on barren sands,
Not shout the harvest-home, when bands
Of reapers dot the meadow-lands?

Thou,—with thy bosom filled with sheaves,
Gathered through toiling morns and eves,
May'st see me glean adust, behind,
Sore-sad of heart that thou shalt bind
    Never again the summer sheaves.

III.

When some dear exile whose sharp pain
    Of banishment we've sickened o'er,
    Is free to seek his patriot shore,
And where his childhood's cheek hath lain,
Sobs out his crazy joy again,—
    Who weeps for grief?—I, even I!
—The wanderer finds his native sky,
The sower counts his garner'd grain,
The banished hails his home again,
    Glad,—thankful,—rapturous: Yet, I sigh
    Inconsolate,—yea, even I!

THE LEGEND OF ATHELNEY.

One desolate, chill December,
   —'Twas hundreds of years ago,—
The moors and the marish fen-lands
   Were dreary and waste with snow:

And fiercely the wolfish tempest
   Howled on the rock-ribb'd shore,
And the heart of the Saxon people
   Was numb to the inmost core.

For the noble and good King Alfred,
   Whose prowess and toils and pains
Had shielded and kept the kingdom,
   And banished the cruel Danes,—

Discomfited now and reaven
   Of province and royal stead,
A nameless fugitive wandered
   Seeking his daily bread.

—'Twas a Yule-tide eve; and the fagots
    That blazed on the earthen floor,
Flung over the bleak morasses
    A glint through the low-brow'd door;—

A glint that across the levels
    Flared like a cresset-light,
That beaconed belated footsteps
    Over the drifts of white.

Cowering beside the embers,
    The King of the Saxon land
Read from the sacred Gospel
    Holden within his hand:—'

Read how the Eastern mages
    Found in the oxen's stall
Jesus the son of Mary,
    The Lord and the King of all;—

Read of the Bethlehem shepherds,—
    Of the strange and marvellous sights
That greeted their upturned faces
    That first of the Christmas-nights.

And the heart of the King was melted,
    And he uttered a lonely sigh;

"A Prince,—yet a houseless exile,—
 An outcast,—even as I!"

But still as he pondered the pages,
 Or ever he was aware,
This tenderest Christmas-story
 Softened his sharp despair.

With a cheerier look he lifted
 His eyes from the beaten floor,
And behold, a gaunt-limb'd beggar
 Sought alms at the wide-set door.

—"Now what is there for bestowal?
 Good mother, beseech thee, see;
For sore is the need that seeketh
 The succor of Athelney."

And the goodwife answered quickly,
 "There is left no dole to make,
Nor a crumb of bread remaineth,
 Save only an oaten cake.

"And the henchmen who seek the forest
 Athwart the dismal wold,
May fail of the wished-for quarry,
 Or perish amid the cold:

"And belike we shall starve, my master—"
"Good mother, I pray, not so!
Who findeth the finch his berries
　　When they're hidden beneath the snow?

"I read in the holy Gospel,—
　　With the story mine eyes are dim,—
That for *us* our Lord left heaven;
　　Is there naught we may do for *Him?*

"When we know that the cruse is empty,
　　And hungry and faint, we feel
'Twixt us and death there is only
　　A morsel of scanty meal,—

"*Then* is the season for giving;
　　And so, for the Lord's sweet sake,
Succor His needy kinsman,
　　Break him the oaten cake:

"Looking to Him to feed us,
　　Sure that the deed is right;
Thankful an act of mercy
　　Can hallow our Christmas-night."

—As asleep on his goat-skin pillow
　　Next morn King Alfred lay,

He dreamed that he talked with Jesus,
    And he hearkened and heard Him say;—

"Now honor be thine, and blessing
    And power and great degree;
Inasmuch to the least thou didst it,
    Thou didst it even to me."

And when in the wintry gloaming
    The dreamer unclosed his eyes,
The vision that met them, filled them
    With a mist of glad surprise.

For there lay on the floor full-antler'd,
    A buck in his fairest prime:
So, with plenty and cheer right royal,
    They welcomed the Christmas-time.

—When spring from the daisied pastures
    Had routed the leaden gloom,
And the reaches of sedgy fen-land
    Were green with the gorse and broom,—

At the head of a new-found army
    King Alfred rode amain,
And hunted from court and castle
    The fierce marauding Dane.

And he hid in his heart the lesson,
  Midst the pride of his high degree,
Which the Christmas-tide had taught him
  In the fens of Athelney.

ALL'S WELL.

"Post number one:—'*All's well.*' Post number two:—'*All's well.*' And so the assuring cry goes the circuit of the camp."—*Officer's Note-Book.*

"ALL'S WELL"—How the musical sound
    Smites, surge-like, the slumbering ear,
  As the sentinel paces his round,
    And carols his tidings of cheer!
Half-startled, the soldier awakes,
    Recalling his senses that roam:
—'Tis only a moment it breaks
    On the dream he was dreaming of home:
        "*All's well!*"

"*All's well!*"—Through the lengthening lines
    Each sentry re-echoes the word,
  And faintly yon forest of pines
    With dreamy responses is stirred:

ALL'S WELL.

On the marge of the nebulous night,
  A wavy, reiterate sigh,
It ripples,—then vanishes quite
  In the infinite deeps of the sky:
          "All's well!"

"All's well!"—In the warfare of life
  Does my soul like a sentinel stand,
Prepared to encounter the strife,
  With well-burnish'd weapon in hand?
While the senses securely repose,
  And doubt and temptation have room,
Does the keen ear of conscience unclose?
  Does she listen, and catch through the gloom:
          "All's well?"

"All's well!"—Can I echo the word?
  Does faith with a sleepless control
Bid the peaceful assurance be heard
  In the questionless depths of my soul?
Then fear not, frail heart!—when the scars
  Of the brave-foughten combat are past,
Clear voices that fall from the stars
  Will quiet thee on to the last:
          "All's well!"

THE SCHOLAR'S HAUNTS.

I.

When the dreaming scholar ponders
    O'er the wondrous tomes of yore,
Till his mind bewildered wanders,
    And his dazed eye heeds no more;—

II.

When with forces spent and jaded,
    And with senses overstrained;
Foiled, eluded and upbraided
    By the phantom-goal ungained;—

III.

When the fever'd spirit flutters
    In some tangled labyrinth caught,
Conscious that the thought it utters
    Leaves unsaid the higher thought;—

IV.

Let him close the misty volume,
  And the crabbèd page of eld;
Life has many a worthier column
  In its unread archives held.

V.

Searching after buried treasures,
  At his feet he overlooks
Simpler wisdom, sweeter pleasures
  Than are prest away in books.

VI.

Not in mansion'd streets whose crowded
  Human tides go roaring by;
Where the brows he meets are clouded,
  And eye answers not to eye:

VII.

Not where false and garish graces
  Mock him with their gilden shows,—
Where unspiritual faces
  Flaunt the lily and the rose:

VIII.

Not where avarice turns its neighbor
  Coldly from the half-shut door;

Not where grind the wheels of labor,
  Can he learn this fresher lore.

IX.

Let him seek the wooded alleys
  Where the flocking ferns abide,
Let him pace the cloistral valleys
  Where the bluest gentians hide:—

X.

Read the lichen-missal'd ledges,—
  Scan the log-books of the streams,—
Till, with thought a-sail, the sedges
  Float him to the land of dreams:

XI.

Mid the forest-porches linger,
  Conning Nature's curious art,
Near enough to lay his finger
  On the pulses of her heart.

XII.

What a tranquil, chasten'd beating!
  Good and ill *there* wage no strife,
Such as surges 'twixt the meeting
  Ebbs and flows of human life.

XIII.

Here he'll breathe the strengthening essence
 Of a purer, loftier clime;
Here he'll learn sublimer lessons
 Than from all the stores of Time.

UNDER THE ELMS.

"So sad it is,"—she said,—and sat her down
  In the old seat;—"So more than sad, to take
  For guide, pale Memory, and retrace again
  With her, the paths the trailing years have worn;
  And in the haunted spots she points us out,
  Wait to recount who sat beside us there,
  And listen while she tells us of the Hours
  That trooped before us hand in hand with Joy.

"How freshly to my sight they stand again,
  Those dear companions of my morning-time,
  In the familiar spots! I seem to hear
  Like a refrain, chime silverly their laughter,
  In rhythmic chorus to their tuneful-hearts:
  The youth with quenchless purpose in his eye;
  The heyday girl, her grace but half unmasked;
  The kind old man whose hands seemed always stretched
  In benediction,—matron'd womanhood,

And gay-eyed, flossy-headed little ones.
I turn to clasp them each, but my strain'd arms
On phantasms close; and only then I find
'Twas a mirage that Memory had evoked
Wherewith to tantalize my crazy vision.
And then upon my cheated heart comes back
With sense too real, that saddest consciousness,
That *only* thus can I behold again,—
Ever again, the faces that are gone!

"Mysteriously,"—she sighed—"an unseen hand
  Cuts at a stroke the thousand precious cords
  Whose twisting Love had labored at for years.
  And they who seemed a portion of ourselves,
  Whose eyes glassed back to us our very thoughts,
  Whose souls we knew by heart, as holy psalms
  Learned from our mother's lips,—are loosed away,
  Snatched out of sight: and in the agony
  And rupture, we forget to look aloft,
  Where the freed spirit has cleaved the open sky,—
  Hugging instead, the cage it left behind.

"And so,"—she said—"for balming of my heart,
  Next it I'll lay this truth: That God's dear hand,
  That spares to waste the smallest filament
  Of beauty that redeems the leaden hue

Of this too-gravely-textur'd weft of ours,
Will gather together at last these golden strands
And weave them, in His marvellous tenderness,
Into the garments that we wear above."

ANTONIO ORIBONI.

I.

In grey Spielburg's dreary fortress, buried from the light of day,
From the bounteous, liberal sunshine, and the prodigal breeze's play,—
Where no human sounds could reach him, save the mocking monotones
Of the sentinel whose footsteps trod the dismal courtyard stones—
Lay the young and knightly victim of the Austrian despot's law,
Worn with slow, consuming sickness, on his meagre bed of straw.

II.

Oft he strove to press his forehead with his pallid hand, in vain,
For the wrist so thin and pulseless could not lift the burdening chain:

Though his lips were parched to frenzy, while the quenchless fever raged,
They had halved the stint of water, lest his thirst might be assuaged;
And because his morbid hunger loathed the mouldy food they thrust
Through the gratings of his dungeon, they had even withheld the crust.

III.

Snatched from country, home and kindred, from his immemorial sky
Rich with summer's lavish leafage, they had flung him here to die;
Not because through perjur'd witness they had stained his noble name,
Not because their jealous malice could adduce one deed of shame;—
But he learned to think that freedom was a guerdon cheaply bought
By the lives of slaughter'd heroes, and . . . he dared to speak the thought!

IV.

And for this,—for *this* they thrust him where no arm might reach to save,
And with youth's hot pulses thronging, sunk him in a living grave:

Strove to stifle in a dungeon under piled centurial
    stone,
Titan-thoughts whose heaving shoulders might upturn
    the tyrant's throne;
—Mother-land! thou heard'st his groaning, and for
    every tear he poured,
Thou hast summoned forth a hero, armed with Free-
    dom's vengeful sword!

V.

Through the dragging years he wasted,—for the flesh
    will still succumb,
Though the inexorable spirit hold the lips sublimely
    dumb,—
And he yearned to clasp his brothers,—enter the old
    trellised door,—
Fall upon his mother's bosom,—kiss his father's hand
    once more,
Till he murmured, as the vision swam before his fever-
    ish eye,—
"O to hear their pitying voices break in blessings ere
    I die!

VI.

"Thou who shrank'st with human shrinking, even as I,
    and thrice did'st pray
If 't were possible the anguish from Thy lips might
    pass away—

Lift this maddening, torturing pressure, seal this struggling, panting breath,—
Let *Thy* mercy cheat man's vengeance,—lead me out to peace through death:
Rend aside this fleshy fastness, shiver this soul-cankering strife,
Turn the key, Thou Blessèd Warder,—break the cruel bolt of life!"

VII.

—In the deep and ghostly midnight, as the lonely captive lay
Gasping in the silent darkness, longing for the dusk of day,
Burst a flood of light celestial through the rayless prison-cell,
And an angel hovering o'er him, toucht his shackles,—and they fell;
And the wondering, trancèd spirit, every thrall of bondage past,
Dropt the shatter'd chains that held it, and sprang upward,—freed at last.

ARTIST-WORK.

WIFE.

"The theme includes a lesson I need to learn;
—Old Leonardo, with his grand grey head
And patriarchal beard, day after day,
Sitting within the Milan market-place,
A-search among that humanest of crowds,
To find some face that he might glorify
With his rare art,—until the rustic hind
Looked from his canvas, a divine Saint John.

"I'll paint the portrait with Correggio's charm
Of light and shade; the meditative brow
Furrowed with thought,—the isolated air,—
The impassive look that masks the life within,—
Till the old Master lives upon my page,
As once among these Milanese. About him
I'll group the common folk that come and go;
The brawny-arm'd, red-turban'd fisherman,—

The chestnut-vender, with his scowling glare,
(A hint of Judas in his sinister eye)—
The mother, who mild-fac'd, looks smiling down,
A possible Madonna, on the child
That grasps her finger:—innocent flower-maidens,
And gossips rusty as the wares they sell.

" 'Twas genius beckoned (I'll show) when Leonardo
Behind him shut, left on the cold, dead wall,—
The forms for which his querulous fancy found
No models, and sought along life's beaten paths
New source of power. I'll make it clear, that he,
Who with unwise, self-centred introspection,
Paints from the airy beings of his brain,
Fails, and is never loyal to the truth;—
That whoso would know aught of Nature's moods,
Must bring his palette forth, and in clear day,
Before her open face, match all his hues,—
The pearly shades of cumulated clouds,
The skyey spaces, tinct with changeful blue,
The mountain dreaming on the horizon's rim,
And all sweet mysteries of this grey-green earth,
Not learned beneath close roofs. Thus will I teach
The lesson thumbed so oft,—that we must look
About our feet for fit material
Wherewith to mould high theme;—that the strait life,
Hemming us round, has rich suggestiveness,—

That even the homeliest office of the hour,
If *duty* but refine and lift it up,
Demanding for its terms of service, small
Renunciations, strict self-disciplines,
Compliances that thwart our inner wish,
—Darling,—*you* there? Ah, I remember now . . .
'The buttons!' My Poem, *Household Priestesses*,
Detained me . . . Why, he's gone without a word!
Below I hear him whistling to his dogs;
Yonder he stops beneath the apple-tree,
Jacket unbutton'd, and his voice drifts thither;
—What is he singing?"

HUSBAND.

"Carolling lark, so high, so high,
          Swallowed in sky,—
  Floating a fairy, airy mote,
  Earthward dropping a liquid note,
        Flutily clear,
Such as it ravishes hearts to hear;

  Out of sight, as a star withdrawn
          Into the dawn,—
  Blotted away from mortal view,
  Drowned in limitless voids of blue,
        Never to be
  Aught but a creature of air to me!

Never to stoop from flight so broad,
                Down to the sod
Where you fashioned a grassy nest;
'Tis too lowly a place of rest:
                Twitterers there,
Chirp, but you heed not, high in air.

Tame little blue-bird, piping sweet,
                Here at my feet,
Merrily chirruping all day long
Only for *me:* With such a song
                Wherefore should I
Care for the warble that floods the sky!"

WIFE.

"Yes,—so man puts it!—Let *him* be the lark
To spring straight upward from the trampled grass,
To fan the dampness from his outstretcht wings,
To leave the wrangling fledglings far below,
And, full abreast the rapturous air, to soar
Unhindered,—wasting all his fervid soul
Upon the heedless breeze; and when, well-tired,
To drop down slowly to the clover-nest,
Where all the hours his mate has fed their brood
In patient love, oblivious of the sky
Or air, or sun!—And who so bold as dare

Make question of the fitnesses of things?
Yet, as true woman and wife, I would far rather
Be a brown sparrow pecking from his hand,
If so it please him best, than even entrance
A thousand other listeners with my song.

"But what, my little scholar? . . . Sigh you too
Over lost buttons?"

CHILD.

"Mother, I am come to ask
   That you'll help me to decline
These '*exceptions:*' Such a task!
   And I cannot read a line.

"What does '*hoc officium*' mean?
   Here is '*facere—to do;*'
With this verb that comes between
   'Tis a puzzle to construe.

"And this mythologic stuff;
   What's the good of it, to know
How ill-natur'd, odious, gruff,
   Those old gods were long ago?

"Then these sums,—they vex me yet,—
   Rule of Two, or Rule of Three,

Which is proper?—I forget,
  For it's quite all one to me.

"What's an equinoctial line?
  What's a zone,—a parallel?
Mother dear, will you define?
  For I'm sure *I* cannot tell!"

MOTHER.

"Come hither, child, and let me kiss all smooth
Those whimpering lips! They win me back again
From the inane ambitions I have nursed,
To graver, holier, purer ministrations
Than service of art. They teach, that cloister'd thought,
Hours winnowed of care, soft-cultur'd, studious ease,
Days hedged from interruption, and withdrawn
Inviolate from household exigence,—
Are not for women,—and least for wives and mothers;
That Leonardo-like, they still must sit
Amidst the jostling stir of clamorous life,
And catch suggestions of the beautiful,
For Love, true Artist, to idealize
In living frescoes on the walls of home."

LEFT BEHIND.

I.

I CANNOT chide away the pain,—
   I cannot bid the throb be still,
That aches and aches through heart and brain,
   And leaves them pulsing to the thrill
Of overmastering memories. They
   Who never saw the eyelids close,
Beneath whose shadowing fringes lay
   All that had given to life repose,
Or charm, or hope, or ease, or joy,
   Or love clear molten from alloy,—
Who have not, tear-blind, watched the breath
   That only breathed to bless them, come
   Slower and fainter, till the dumb
Unanswering lips grew white with death,—
They cannot know, by grief untaught,
   What an unfathomed depth I find,
Of ebbless anguish in the thought
   That I am left behind.

II.

What matters it that other eyes
   Have smiles to give me just as sweet,
   Or softly other tongues repeat
Endearments of as gentle guise?
I only feel that whatsoe'er
   Its melting tenderness may be,
'Tis not the smile whose gracious cheer
   Was more than all the world to me:
I only feel though winning-kind
   Is every word that voice may say,
   'Tis not the one that passed away
When I was left behind.

III.

I know,—I know that as of yore,
   Nature is festive in her mirth;
That still the sunshine shimmers through
The infinite, palpitating blue,
   As goldenly as heretofore:
I know this green and billowy earth
   Tides underneath the smile of God,
As to the moonlight tides the sea;
—I'm wounded by the mocking glee,
   I'm hurt by all the joy abroad.

LEFT BEHIND.

The smiting blow that grief has given,
So jars the mirror of my mind,
  That everything of sweet or fair,
  Has but distorted reflex there;
And O the tears,—the tears, like rain
Upon its surface leave their stain,
  Since my Belovéd went to heaven,
Since I was left behind!

IV.

There is a Hand that can restore
  The spirit's equipoise, till true,
In faith's unwavering light once more,
  His image trembles back to view.
Dear Christ!—when there Thy form appears,
Let me not blot it with my tears,
  That are not murmuring tears, though sad;
I would be patient,—I would find
  How much the thought can reconcile,
Can lift me up and make me glad,
  That only for a little while
Shall I be left behind.

THE BELLS OF BRIENNE.*

The setting sun was slanting red
   Across the battle plain,
As slackening bit, the Emperor
   Surveyed the heaps of slain.

He gazed with hard, impassive eye
   Upon the carnage spread,
Nor made account of dying moans,
   Nor saw the piled-up dead.

No thought of thousand widow'd wives
   Awoke remorseful fear;
No sobs of wailing orphans filled
   His apathetic ear.

—'Twas but the common fate of war,
   Whose tempest-shock of wrath

* Napoleon was educated at the military school of Brienne.

Foredoomed that human wreck and waste
  Must strew the conqueror's path.

If million lives alone sufficed
  To rear the pile so high
That he might climb to boundless power,
  —Then let the million die.

A-sudden, broke a peal of bells,
  Startling the feverish air,
That clanged across the bloody field
  The vesper-call to prayer.

The victor in his saddle drooped
  With quick, spasmodic start,
As if a whizzing random shot
  Had smote him at the heart.

Those bells! . . . What long-forgotten hours,
  What careless school-boy times,
What rush of innocent happiness,
  All mocked him in their chimes!

And who dare say, as contrast sharp
  Pierced with its stab of pain,—
He had not given crown,—empire,—all,
  To be a boy again!

For when he turned erect once more,
   To praise the cannoniers
Who won the fight that day,—they saw
   His cheek was wet with tears.

PROEM.

To "Silverwood—a book of memories."

Turning tearfully the pages
  Of the By-gone's blotted lore,
—Palimpsests o'erwrit with records
  Of the luminous heretofore;

Records where a gleam of brightness,
  Through the fresher sorrow shines;
Records with a throb of heart-break
  Troubling all the wavering lines;

I have gathered of the beauty
  That emblazons still the book,
Here, some grace's half-blurr'd outline,—
  There, some hint of tone or look:

Transcripts, ah, how faint, Belovéd!
  Dim suggestions of that rare
Inner realm the world around you
  Never knew was hidden there.

Like the spies of old, I've entered,
   Searching all the richest parts,
Bringing back some grapes of Eshcol
   From the Canaan of your hearts.

For I need the wine of solace
   Which their vintage-tide supplies,—
Need the omer's strengthening manna
   Meted to me from the skies.

Sad, behind the wains full-laden,
   Memory, like a gleaner, strives
Thus to gather up a handful
   From the harvest of your lives.

Seeking in her tender patience,
   Through the corn-land's cast-off leaves,
Golden grains of sweet refreshment
   Shaken from the garner'd sheaves.

If she has not filled her bosom
   With the wealth of ripened ears,
'Twas because her eyes were clouded,
   And she could not see for tears!

LITTLE JEANIE'S SLEEP.

. . . How tired she was growing!—It may be
  God pitied so tender a sight,
And whispered,—"You're weary, my baby,
  So shut your sweet eyes, and good-night!"

And she shut them. Be sure that our Father
  Who guards every step that they tread,
Knows better than we when to gather
  The little tired sleepers to bed.

And lying there now, midst the rarest
  Of jasmines and snow-drops so white,
Herself the delightsomest, fairest
  That ever unsheathed in our sight,—

Midst the blossoms she loved in such fashion
  As God loves, proclaiming them "good,"—
In your hunger of ravenous passion,
  Would you wake her to life,—if you could?

If out the blue glory above you,
   The voice of the Highest were heard,
"One word,—and you have her to love you
   Again," . . . would you utter the word?

Nay, never! The perfected seven
   Sweet years of her sojourn below,
Were balmed with the breezes of heaven,
   But would it have always been so?

Like the silverest sunbeam of morning
   Your hearts through her promise were blest;
Would you hazard the tokens of warning
   That point to the clouds in the west?

O say it was well, ere the splendor
   Of her dawning had died into grey,
While the rose-dew of childhood was tender,
   She should glide through the arches of day.

O say that her sleep is *not* dreary:
   It only was kindest and best,
That her Father who saw she was weary,
   Should wrap her the sooner to rest.

THE UNATTAINED.

THE loftiest-soaring thoughts that ever find
Within our souls their transient nestling-place,
Elude most subtly the detaining grasp
Wherewith gross speech would hold them.
                                      Oftentimes
Through the pure æther of our silent souls
The warble swells, scarce audible, scarce perceived,
Yet circling still with clearer utterance
Lower and nearer, till it drops straight down
Into our heart. And then in eager haste
To keep our lark a captive fast, that so
Some other ear may hear what we have heard,
We plait a cage about with nicest art,—
We net the very goldenest of our gyves,
And all being done, feel after the rare singer,
When lo, 'tis gone! Full consciously secure,
We tarried overlong, and the quick thought,
Too airy for our snare, has safe escaped;
And far receding, high above and higher,

Through the mind's radiant atmosphere, we catch
What evermore we fail to others' sense
To make articulate. Some ruffled down
Snatched all too rudely from the silvery breast,—
Some feather azure-tipt, caught from the wings
Spread out of sight, alone are left to prove
The presence of the singer in our souls.

THE HALLOWED NAME.

I.

A THOUSAND times I've rung it out
  With laughter's lightest tone;
And heard it tossed from lip to lip
  As jocund as my own:
But now with hushing tenderness
  I fold and wrap it round,
As if I grudged that air profane
  Should share the sacred sound.

II.

If unawares it strikes my ear,
  Beneath the blow I start;
And swift, concentric thrills suffuse
  The quiet of my heart:
All other visions break before
  That circle's widening sway,
Till on the outmost bourn of tears
  My memories melt away.

III.

O love that flung it, music-fraught,
  Upon the zestful air,—

O grief that sobs it with the slow,
    Awed sanctity of prayer,—
Ye know I may not moan it forth
    With less of reverent breath
Than trembles o'er the mouth we kiss,
    Made consecrate by death!

IV.

Within a far-off place of graves,
    Midst other names unknown,
Strange eyes behold it lettered out
    On love's memorial stone:
They syllable with questioning lips
    The simple, brief-drawn line;
But through what gusts of voiceless tears
    It had been kissed by mine.

V.

Yet on a tablet deeper cut,
    I keep that silent word,
Which in the haunts of living men
    Shall nevermore be heard:
Too pure for common uses,—raised
    High o'er all praise or blame:
Yea,—since they've learned it up in heaven,
    It *is* a hallowed name!

DANTE IN EXILE.

"What wilt thou?" asked the Prior: and the stranger looking steadfastly at him only answered, "*Peace.*"

PEACE for the exile banished from his home,
Familiar kindred, and dear native land?—
Peace for the man whose birth-soil roots him out
With scoffs, and flings him like a noxious weed
To shrivel and scorch in sultry heats of scorn.
Yea,—even for *him;* if that his fiery soul
Can find in wholesome and indignant hate,
A nutriment whose bitter strength can still
All gentler cravings. But no "peace" for thee,
O Poet, with thy marvellous organism,
Sweet as Ravenna's rathest summer-rose,—
Soft as a rivulet mid Arezzo's hills;
Yet stern and rugged as the hard-bol'd fir,
Or blasting as Vesuvius, belching fire;
With thine austere and virile soul, attempered
With woman-like lovingness, and thy great heart

Thy strong, heroic, melancholy heart,
In its refinement of ecstatic pain
Evermore quivering;—ah, no "peace" for thee!

No alien fields of blue could ever seem
As living as thine own Etrurian skies:
No stream could wake, how bright soe'er its flash,
The grave, still joy that thy young years had known
By silvery Arno:—never city show
Such queenliness of proud magnificence,
As beautiful Florence lying like a bride
In the caresses of her oliv'd hills.
Yet *she* could thrust thee out,—yet she could bear
To bind thy chivalrous spirit to the rack
Of most ingenious torture, till thy life
Of heart-break wore at last away: And thou
Couldst grandly tame thy seething nature down,
And with superb forgiveness,—such as saints
Learn only in heaven,—still love her with a love
Inordinate, quenchless, unappeasable,
Throughout the eating years of martyrdom!

She could not take thine all. Though sad athirst
For sympathies gracious as had once refreshed
Thy Tuscan home,—thou hadst a secret spring,
Healing, exhaustless, whence thy royal soul
Drew strength and solace midst its harshest woes:

And even in thy most desolate poverty
Of hope and comfort, thou, with affluent hand,
Didst pour from that divinest fount of song,
Delicious waters, that were evermore
To be *her* pride who scorned thee!
      But the stream,
The deep, pure, living Hippocrene that sends
Down the long ages, draughts that bear refreshment
To myriads of hot lips,—could never cure
Thine own home-sickness,—could not satisfy
Thy harrowing yearnings. And the boon of peace
Which thou hadst sought through lonely wanderings,—
Through years of aching banishment, in vain,
Thy haunted heart found only in the grave.

THE VISION OF THE SNOW.

I.

"She has gone to be with the angels;"
    So they had always said
To the little questioner asking
    Of his fair, young mother, dead.

II.

They never had told of the darkness
    Of the sorrowful-silent tomb,
Nor scared the sensitive spirit
    By linking a thought of gloom

III.

With the girl-like, beautiful being,
    Who patiently from her breast,
Had laid him in baby-sweetness,
    To pass to her early rest.

IV.

And when he would lisp—"Where is she?"
  Missing the mother-kiss,
They answered—"Away in a country
  That is lovelier far than this;

V.

"A land all a-shine with beauty
  Too pure for our mortal sight,
Where the darling ones who have left us
  Are walking in robes of white."

VI.

And with eagerest face he would listen,
  His tremulous lips apart,
Till the thought of the Beautiful Country
  Haunted his yearning heart.

VII.

—One morn, as he gazed from the window,
  A miracle of surprise,
A marvellous, mystic vision
  Dazzled his wondering eyes.

VIII.

Born where the winter's harshness
  Is tempered with spring-tide glow,

The delicate Southern nursling
Never had seen the snow.

IX.

And clasping his childish fingers,
  He turned with a flashing brow,
And cried—"We have got to heaven . . .
  Show me my mother now!"

OUT OF THE SHADOW.

I.

"Life is so beautiful,"—I said,
　"In the young, misty morning's prime,
　—And yours is just at blossom-time;
The sparkles hang about your head,
And all the gracious bounty shed
　Lavish above your sixteen years,
Wears its first freshness still; and yet,
　Sweet daughter, have I seen no tears,
Nor caught an unawares regret
Deepening the softness of your eye,—
Is it so easy, then, to die?"

II.

(I always knew my darling's face
Showed saintly through its utmost grace
Of pure expression, but her brow
Had something lambent round it now.)

III.

"*If* life is beautiful,"—she said,
　"Where everything its beauty mars,

What must it be above the stars,
  Where all its greatening powers are fed
  For evermore with angels' bread?
And often, when I wake at night,
  And watch the sky in musings fond,
Made to hide heaven, and yet so bright,
  I think . . . what must it be beyond?
And I can scarce keep down the prayer
Of inward longing to be there."

IV.

(O sweet, child-love that did not mark
The infinite vague of pathless dark
That lay betwixt those leaping eyes
And the home-windows in the skies!)

V.

"Still,—life *is* beautiful,"—I said:
  "Even while I take the medicin'd cup
    God's hand hath mixed, and drink it up,—
Even while with soul disquieted
Through gnawing care and doubt and dread,
Life still is beautiful! . . . and Death—
  How *can* Death seem an angel when
He takes away my name and breath
  Out of the land of living men?
O child, the faith is strong to save
That makes such compact with the grave!"

VI.

(A wondrous radiance glowed upon
  The mouth that closed to meet my kiss;
Surely the glory that Saint John
  Beheld in Patmos, was like this!)

VII.

"Still *Death* is beautiful,"—she said,
  "A beckoning seraph in whose arms
  I safer sink from all alarms,
Than when, a frighten'd child, I fled
And sobbed my fears and hid my head
On your warm bosom. Mother sweet,
  My Lord hath broken His heart for me,
That mine break not; then is it meet,
  That when His messenger should be
Sent on the errand full of balm,
—'Come and be with me where I am!'
I who have often longed to go,
Should shrink to greet His servant so?"

VIII.

(He came;—I felt she saw him stand
  Before her, in the pallid dawn;
One eager start,—one outstretcht hand . . .
  And then I knew my child was gone!)

THE DIFFERENCE.

I.

A BIRD within the alders sang
   A rapturous song;
So tearful-sweet its quavers rang,
   Now soft,—now strong,—
That on my ravisht ear the strain
   Began to ache,
Till, wrung with too delicious pain,
   My heart did break.
But when, obedient to the call
   That drew me on,
I flew to own the mystic thrall
Of the subduing madrigal,
   —The bird was gone!
And from some other alder-bough
   His liquid throat
Pours forth the grieving ripples now,
   That swell and float,
And break with ecstasy divine
Some heart as foolish-fond as mine!

II.

Man's love,—I sighed,—is such a strain
   Of capturing power,—
The nest in which the dove hath lain
   One throbbing hour:
Woman's . . . the soul that listeneth,
With overborne, enchanted breath,—
The hope that never perisheth,—
The life that does not die with death.

ALONE.

A LITTLE child whose rhythms of laughter smoothed
All household dissonance away,—whose step
Kept time to the light measure of her heart,—
Whose frolic-nature claimed all kindredship
With jestful, jubilant things, lay piteously
Moaning, held in the grasp of mortal pain.

The sportive look died out within her eyes,
The quip upon her tongue, the mirthfulness
From the young voice, as the sunshiny path,
Where danced with her the fairy-footed hours,
Darkened beneath the sudden shadow that came
Stalking between her and life's new-risen sun.

She raised a troubled glance: "What is it, father?"
And he made answer; "Only a messenger
Whom the dear Lord hath sent to call you, Sweet,
Away from all things sad, to a fair land
Where it is always beautiful summer-time."
Startled,—about the stooping neck she clung

With passionate burst of childlike uncontrol:
"Go with me, father, for I am afraid;
I shiver at the creeping of the dark;
I tremble! Let me hold your dear, warm hand;
O father . . . not alone! Why even here
About this pretty world I have not ventured
To walk untended—"

"Little trembler, no,—
You shall not go untended. Christ himself
Has travelled the pathway through, and made it bright;
And now He leaves the seraph-songs a little,
To come and hold my tender baby's hand:
And just outside the dusk,—(some call it, death)—
He waits to bear you past the shady places,
Up to your mother, darling, where she leans
And watches for you at the gates of pearl
We've talked about right often: With Him so close,
You will not be afraid?"

The searching eyes
Closed as if weighted by too heavy a thought;
And in a silence, solemn and strange to see,
She lay as grappling with a truth that mastered
Her little powers. But when again she turned
Upon her father her full eyes, the fear
Had vanisht, and the radiant look of joy
Came back to brighten her face, just as of old;

And from her mouth ashened to deathliness,
Faltered consent articulate, which to him
Whose ear caught at its broken meaning, seemed
The first, faint trial-note of that glad song
Which the sweet baby-voice should sing for ever.

SAINT CECILIA.

I.

HAVEN'T you seen her?—and don't you know
Why I dote on the darling so?
Let me picture her as she stands
There with the music-book in her hands,
Looking as ravishing, rapt and bright
As a baby Saint Cecilia might,
Lisping her bird-notes,—that's Belle White.

II.

Watch as she raises her eyes to you,
Half-crusht violets dipt in dew,
Brimming with timorous, coy surprise,—
(Doves have just such glistening eyes:)
But, let a dozen of years have flight,
Will there be *then* such harmless light
Warming these luminous eyes,—Belle White?

III.

Look at the pretty, feminine grace
Even now, on the small, young face:

Such a consciousness as she speaks,
Flushing the ivory of her cheeks,—
Such a maidenly, arch delight
That she carries me captive quite,
Snared with her daisy-chain,—Belle White.

IV.

Many an ambusht smile lies hid
Under that innocent, downcast lid:
Arrows will fly, with silvery tips,
Out from the bow of those arching lips
Parting so guilelessly, as she stands
There with the music-book in her hands,
Chanting her bird-notes soft and light,
Even as Saint Cecilia might,
Dove with the folded wings,—Belle White!

THE APOSTLE OF TRUTH,

WHO DENIED HIS MASTER.

(*"E pur si muove."*)

WHY bade he not blind Error bring
   Its hate to light the pyre,
While he stood wrapped with grand disdain,
   In martyr-robes of fire?
He knew no links could bind the soul
   Whose venturous courage trod,
Unpiloted through pathless voids,
   The infinite of God!

From its far, eyried crest of power
   The eagle-spirit swooped;
Yet at the mumbling beck of Eld,
   With weak compliance stooped;
While Superstition wrought and strove
   To rivet fast the chain,
Lest that too dauntless wing should mount
   The dangerous heights again.

"The Holy-Office cells are grim,"—
　　Succumbing flesh could say;
Though spirit whispered,—"There's a light
　　Diviner than the day."
—"But when resistless hands oppose,
　　And myriad tongues deny,
What can I else?"—"The grandest thing . . .
　　For Truth's sake,—dare to die!"

Strange!—that the ray which filled his soul
　　With utmost floods of light,
Should even one cowering moment lose
　　Its radiance to his sight:
Strange!—that the eye whose ken could pierce
　　To worlds on worlds afar,
Should let a dastard film of fear
　　Hide truth's resplendent star.

THE OPEN GATE.

PAST and over;—Yet no frenzy
  Racks my overladen brain;
Grief can anodyne the spirit,
  Woe can numb its pain.

Did you deem the blow would crush me,
  Pitying comforters,—that I
In despairing acquiescence
  Could but moan and die?

Nay,—one deadening shock hath palsied
  So my sentient nature o'er,
Well I knew no after sorrow
  Now could craze me more.

Yet I grasped without abatement
  Its full meaning when ye said
Softly, lest the sound should stun me,
  That the child was dead.

Keep that bitterer word,—it gauges
  Something of that *other* woe,
Different as the soundless ocean's
  From the shallows' flow.

O, not dead:—*that* word has in it
  Maddening terrors, wild alarms:
—Rather, God has given the darling
  To his father's arms!

Months,—or is it years?—have vanisht
  Since for *him* the boy has smiled,
And if saints can long in heaven,
  He must want the child.

. . . I have seen the gates unfolding,
  (Heavenly hath the vision been,)
—Seen the little stranger venture
  Through the radiance in:

Watched the timid, shrinking wonder
  On the baby-face so fair,
And the kindling smile of rapture,
  When he found *him* there:

Watched the soul-full recognition;
  Saw the finger pointing back

To the arms he knew were stretching
　Toward that shining track:

Till I wondered at my sorrow,—
　But the vision would not stay;
And it left the truth unsoftened,
　—He is taken away.

—What is left me? Only patience,
　Only heart to watch and wait,
Till that moment when as convoys
　From the open gate,

Forth shall issue child and father,
　Bend above me,—name my name,—
Sent upon a tenderer errand
　Than they ever came:

If to nurse the thought can lighten
　Even now the crush of woe,
Surely, surely 'twill be blissful
　To arise and go!

THE RESTING-PLACE.

As palmers wont to hail the nichéd seat
At desert-well, where they put off the shoon
And robe of travel,—so I, a pilgrim as they,
Tired with my six-days' track, would turn aside
Out of the scorch and glare into the shade
Of Sunday-stillness. Resting, I would listen
Gladdened, to the gurgle of the hidden stream,
Till every fevered throb grew calm through peace.
So sitting, that perfectest repose should steal
Inward, which disillusionizes sense,
And leaves the spirit, unhindered of the flesh,
Free to forget itself in dreams of heaven.

I would inhale the bracing, zested air
That vivifies the soul and lifts it up
To saintly heights: and to my lips that crave
Refreshment cooler than lies ever staled

In cisterns choked by weedy worldliness,
I'd carry in my scallop of faith, the water
That gushes from the Smitten Rock.
                        And thus
Strengthened, I would take up my staff again,
And with reanimate and quickened step,
Sing *Benedicite,* and go my way.

THE RAIN-DROP'S FATE.

Its home was the breast of a luminous rack
   Whose fringes of purple and dun
Were frayed by a gust on its turbulent track,
   And tangled by shafts from the sun.

Slow drifted the cloud in the wane of the light,
   Till it hung o'er a garden so fair,
That the rain-drop grew envious-sad at the sight,
   And peevishly sighed to be there.

A lover-like breeze that came out of the south,
   Snatched up from its fretful repose
The murmurer, and laid it,—first kissing its mouth,—
   In the innermost heart of a rose.

The chamber with crimson-wrought tapestry hung,
   The floor sanded over with gold,

The fragrance spilt out of the censers that swung
  Around, were a joy to behold.

The saffron-dyed rift in the distance afar,
  Seemed only a blot on the night,
And the jubilant rain-drop looked out on a star
  In a trance of exulting delight.

'Twas the bliss of a moment: A tender-browed girl
  Slow threading through pathway and bower,
Bade the eye she drew after her, look at the pearl
  That swam in the heart of the flower.

"Not the Queen of the East had so perfect a draught,
  Nor a chalice so jewel'd to sip,"—
He said, as he gave her the rose-cup:—she quaffed,
  And the pearl was dissolved on her lip.

ROSALIE.

I.

The bickering fire-light dances
   About the fragrant room,
And the windows' crimson drapery
   Shuts out the twilight-gloom:
And the swell and fall of music
   Make preludes to the mirth
Of storied voice and happy heart
   Around the blazing hearth:
            —But Rosalie
Heeds not the ballad, nor the burst
            Of childish glee.

II.

The wintry wind is shrieking
   Like some wild thing in wrath,
And snaps the hoary beechen-boughs,
   And stamps them in its path.

And as with stridulous bellow
  The surge of sleety rain
Comes booming with tornado-strength
  Against the window-pane,—
        Sad Rosalie
Shades off the light, and sends her thoughts
        Far out to sea.

III.

And while her troubled forehead
  Against the pane is prest,
A dizzy rush of eddying fears
  Goes swirling through her breast.
—She sees a struggling vessel
  Poised on a mountain wave;
She looks again. . . . 'Tis fathoms plunged
  Within a billowy grave!
With wandering aim her fingers
  Close, with a pallid start,
Upon a hidden tress that feels
  The quickening of her heart:
        For Rosalie
Shivers to think what sunny heads
        Go down at sea.

IV.

Amidst the merry pauses,
  The blast is louder heard;

And a child whose sudden sympathy
  By danger's sense is stirred,—
Whispers with blue eyes glazing,
  And roses blanched to white,
"*O Sister !—think how many ships*
  The storm will wreck to-night !"
—The anguish only needed
  That touch of pity more
To crown its torture:—the light form
  Slides fainting to the floor.
          Ah, Rosalie !
—*That* night the twin-locks floated deep
          Beneath the sea !

THE AMULET.

I.

The braided circlet clasps her arm,
  And midst the jewels rare,
The light is trembling with the charm
  That holds it captive there.

Tranced with the flashing ruby-gleams,
  Cloud-pillowed it will lie,
And utter forth in tell-tale dreams
  Its secret to the sky.

II.

But purer links than these, inwove
  With yet a subtler art,
Set with that burning, brilliant, love,
  Are wound about her heart.

Thought lingers, kindling at the glance,
  And though it owns no thrall,
There gathers o'er her eye's expanse
  A haze that tells him all.

THE IDLE LYRE.

THERE was an idle lyre
   Amid Heaven's choral band;
A messenger was summoned
   To hear his Lord's command,
That from earth's lowly children
   Some favored one he bring,
Who had a skillful finger
   To sweep the golden string.

O high—O, wondrous honour!
   Whose shall the glory be
To break that lyre's strange silence
   With heaven-born harmony?
What mighty laurel'd minstrel,
   First of the fame-wreath'd throng,
Shall angels reckon worthy
   To swell those waves of song?

Some calm and saintly spirit?
   Some affluent soul whose praise

Hath caught the sacred key-note
  That seraph voices raise?
Some pure unearthly nature,—
  Some listening heart that hears,
In golden-centred silence,
  The music of the spheres?

—A little child was playing
  Beside his mother's knee,
Clad in the simple meekness
  Of infant purity:
The angel smiling, beckoned,
  And breathed the soft behest:
The lowliest one could waken
  That silent lyre the best.

POWERS' PROSERPINE.

THAT half-averted face,—It takes my breath!
The smile that drifts around the dimpled mouth,
Tears eddying in it; the low, broadened brow,
Calm through its passionless divinity,
The cheek whose velvet softness seems to dint,
As a thought touches it; the floss of hair,
A Juno-circlet round the imperial head;
The chastened charm of maiden modesty
Pleading in every curve, and welling up
In tided heavings of the cloven breasts:
—What marvel that the cluster'd loveliness
Should tempt a kingly spirit from his throne!

Ascend, successful Master, farther still
The path that upward leads: Take thou the torch
—Than Ceres' brighter,—which thy genius lights
At its own Etna-fire, to guide thee on,
And in thy beauty-quest, search o'er the world.
Outstrip the Grecian in his marvellous craft;

Shake in the grasp of Angelo the palm;
Receive the chisel from Canova's hand,
And catch Thorwaldsen's mantle as it falls;
Then humbled turn away from earth's poor Art,
Confessing that its grandest skill is only
The dust of the balance weighed against *His* power
Who fashioned with a word a perfect man,
And breathed into the clay a living soul!

LIFE-CLOSE.

I.

The calm, full day, so flusht with light,
  So arched with azur'd majesty,
  Has sunk beneath the mystic sea
That shuts the immortal from our sight.

II.

And as we watched its westering rays
  Go down behind the purple rim,
  We dared not let a tear-drop dim
That rich horizon's lustrous blaze.

III.

What kingly promise spanned its morn;—
  What noble ends its noon-time hours!
  How grandly its unresting powers
Have all the heat and burden borne!

IV.

'Tis well the longed-for night should come
With curtain-drop of kind release;
So, in our souls we whispered—"Peace,"
As the last shadows settled home.

V.

But while we miss the shining bars
That compassed round this day so bright,
We look aloft,—and lo, the night
Darkening above us, throbs with stars!

THE BY-GONE.

(A Southern Christmas Carol.)

I.

The dear Twenty-Fifth of December,
   The festival fullest of joy,
Most precious for age to remember,
   Most merry for maiden and boy,—
Comes again with its promise to gladden,
   Comes again with its prodigal cheer,
To banish whatever may sadden
   The lingering days of the year.

II.

We know that this beautiful season
   Is flung like a garland of mirth
(We thank the dear Lord for the reason!)
   All over the face of the earth:

The homeliest cottage seems brighter,
   The wintriest spirit less sad;
The greyest of landscapes grows lighter,
   And the world's wrinkled forehead is glad.

III.

'Tis the time of all times to remember
   The past, and be happy:—and yet
The shadow that glooms *our* December
   Is,—to feel that we cannot forget!
We heap the red fagots together,—
   We wrap us with carefulest art;
But the cold's not the cold of the weather,
   The rime is the rime of the heart.

IV.

All the length of our desolate border
   The hopeless make moan,—and alas,
In the conflict of order with order,
   The peoples are withered like grass.
No light-hearted, loud jubilation
   Makes the holiday hearty with glee:
A hush broods abroad the plantation,
   Like the storm's dying sob on the sea!

V.

There once was a time,—let us cherish
   Its memory deep in the core

Of emotions we dare not let perish,—
    A time we can look for no more!
Let us tell to our children the story,
    With earnest and tremulous mouth,
Of the sweetness, the grace and the glory
    That hallowed the Homes of the South.

VI.

Let us picture the Christmas-tide blisses,
    The holly-crown'd hall,—the brave cheer,—
The warm, courtly welcome,—the kisses
    Of the kindred unmet for a year:—
The throngs of old servants who gather
    To witness the dance and the glee;
This dandled our mother,—our father
    That patriarch nursed on his knee.

VII.

The eyes of our children will glisten
    Half tearful, half doubtful, perchance;
And they'll think that it sounds, as they listen,
    Like the page of a feudal romance.
And thus, from our loving lips learning
    The By-gone so tenderly o'er,
They will sigh with regretfulest yearning
    For the beautiful Christmas of yore.

1865.

IN PACE.

I.

MOTHER, drooping wan and weary
In the midnight silence dreary,
Conning o'er the childish prattle
Of the boy who fell in battle,
Till your memories sting you,—sighing,
—"Who will tell me where he's lying?"

Dry your tears now: kindly faces
Bend above the hallowed places,—
Seek the nameless dead, and bear them
Home to tombs their hands prepare them;
—Friend, compatriot, comrade, brother,
And your boy's among them, mother.

II.

Widowed wife, whose heart is breaking
Slowly, surely with its aching,

Moaning on your tear-stained pillow,
—"Were his grave beneath the willow
In the church-yard,—kneeling by it,
I could sob myself to quiet:"

Henceforth calm your heartache: tender
Patriot love doth solace render;
Plants the cypress,—rears the column,
And with saintly rites and solemn
Lays your darling there: Pale weeper,
Go and pray beside your sleeper.

III.

Maiden, with white lids dropt slowly
Over eyes downcast and holy,
Hiding grief that none discover
For the far-off-buried lover,—
Wailing of that spot so lonely,
—"O, to kiss and clasp it only!"

Be your voiceless sorrow softened;
Think of him no more uncoffined:
Not a tended turf is greener,
Not a cedarn copse serener,
Not a mossier mound than this is;
Maiden, warm it with your kisses!

SONNETS.

EQUIPOISE.

Just when we think we've fixed the golden mean,—
   The diamond point, on which to balance fair
   Life and life's lofty issues,—weighing there,
With fractional precision, close and keen,
Thought, motive, word and deed,—there comes between
   Some wayward circumstance, some jostling care,
   Some temper's fret, some mood's unwise despair,
To mar the equilibrium, unforeseen,
   And spoil our nice adjustment!—Happy he,
Whose soul's calm equipoise can know no jar,
   Because the unwavering hand that holds the scales,
Is the same hand that weighed each steadfast star,—
   Is the same hand that on the sacred tree
Bore, for his sake, the anguish of the nails!

SATURDAY NIGHT.

The spirit's trailing garments that have swept
   Through all the week along the dusty way,
   Catching assoilment from the griming day,
(Though oft aside the foot in voidance stept,—)
Gather them up to-night: they have not kept
   Immaculate their whiteness from the clay;
   The delicate weftage, fretting troubles fray;
The broider'd hem, oft caught by cares that crept
Brier-like, along the path,—is rent apart,
Ravelled and distained. Wherefore, disheartened one,
Loosen these work-day vestments from thee, lest,
Uncleansed by meditation's holy art,
   Thy soul be found unfitted to put on
The pure, fair linen of the Sabbath rest.

CONVIVA SATUR.

If *he* could say it, turning from the board
  His creedless life had spread him, nor repine
  That in his dear Digentia, other wine
Than his, should gather coolness, or the hoard
Of Sabine olives be for others stored,—
  Then surely, I! The love this heart of mine
  Knew of all draughts to be the most divine,
Into life's crystal goblet hath been poured
  Till it runs over: faith, the living bread,
  Hallows the table, while on every side,
With heaping clusters have my hopes been fed,
  Nor tempered appetite been once denied:
And I am ready, when the thanks are said,
To rise and leave the banquet,—satisfied.

THE MORROW.

Of all the tender guards which Jesus drew
  About our frail humanity, to stay
  The pressure and the jostle that alway
Are ready to disturb, whate'er we do,
And mar the work our hands would carry through,—
  None, more than this, environs us each day
With kindly wardenship:—"Therefore, I say,
  Take *no* thought for the morrow." Yet we pay
  The wisdom scanty heed, and impotent
  To bear the burden of the imperious Now,
Assume the future's exigence unsent.
  God grants no overplus of power: 'Tis shed
Like morning manna: Yet we dare to bow
And ask,—"Give us to-day our *morrow's* bread!"

DOUBT.

I LIFT weak hands in lowliest thankfulness,
   That, as a little stumbling child who knows
   Naught of the way he treads, but onward goes,
Happy, secure, unquestioning, reasonless,
Because he feels his father's fingers press
   His own in steadfast guidance,—doubts impose
No cross-lights to confuse me or distress.
"*Is* this the way?" If Christ but answer,—"Yes,"—
I am content. I would not have the trust
   Of yearling prattlers shame me, while I stand
   Demanding *how* the bridgeless gulf is crossed,—
The scaleless mountain levelled with the dust,—
The mist-swathe rent in which the path seems lost;
   What need to ask?—*My Father holds my hand.*

OURS.

Most perfect attribute of love, that knows
   No separate self,—no conscious *mine* nor *thine;*
   But mystic union, closer, more divine
Than wedded soul and body can disclose.
No flush of pleasure on thy forehead glows,
No mist of feeling in thine eyes can shine
   No faintest pain surprise thee, but there goes
The lightning-spark along love's viewless line,
   Bearing with instant message to my heart,
Responsive recognition. Suns or showers
   May come between us; silences may part;
The rushing world know not, nor care to know;—
Yet back and forth the flashing secrets go,
   Whose sacred, only sesamé is,—*ours!*

THE HYSSOP.

BEAR me no lordly palm-branch, such as waves
   Triumphantly in conquering hands, nor choose
   The crown of bay, pearled with Olympian dews,
Nor fadeless laurel, such as poet craves:
Twine me no myrtle which the lover laves
   With passion's tears; wreathe not the mournful yew's
   Funereal bough, nor marvel I refuse
The willow drooping low o'er hallow'd graves,
   Nor bind me yet the peaceful olive's leaves.
But grant me dearer, holier far than all
   Emblems of earthly good or earthly loss,
That sign of heavenliest boon the soul receives,—
   The lowly-springing hyssop of the wall,
Wet with the blood that flows from Calvary's cross!

NATURE'S LESSON.

PAIN is no longer pain when it is past;
   And what is all the mirth of yesterday,
   More than the yester flush that paled away,
Leaving no trace across the landscape cast
   Whereby to prove its presence there? The blast
That bowed the knotted oak beneath its sway,
And rent the lissome ash, the forest may
   Take heed of longer, since strewn leaves outlast
Strewn sunbeams even. Be thou like Nature then,
   Calmly receptive of all sweet delights,
The while they soothe and strengthen thee: and when
   The wrench of trial comes with swirl and strain,
Think of the still progressive days and nights,
   That blot with equal sweep, both joy and pain.

THE STIRRED NEST.

Too much on earth,—too much on what must sway
  With every oversweeping gust of time,
  I've set my hopes, where no rude care might climb,
Fond thought!—to spoil my nest or steal away
The cherished singers that for many a day
  Had cheered me with their song. But the rough wind
Again and yet again has wrenched the bough,
  And driven my clinging fledglings far and wide,
To wail the refuge which they fail to find,
  And fill my ear with plaintive moaning now.
Where shall the scattered, homeless wanderers hide
  And build once more? Not here, where storms are
    rife,—
Not here, my heart!—but where no ills betide,
  In the safe shelter of the Tree of Life!

THE REASON.

WHEN Death, that irremediable ill,
   Soothed only by submission's bitter balm,
   Wrests from our souls remorselessly, their calm,
Sweet, natural joys,—we deem no peace can fill,
   Nor zest can stimulate, nor hope have skill
To solace them more. We say, the soothing psalm
Will henceforth ever seem a dirge:—"I am
   The Resurrection and the Life,"—be still
   Muffled by falling clods, whereon our tears
So idly rain. When bowed the ancient sage
   Above his dead, surprised with anguish deep,
"It cannot help thee,"—urged the friends whose fears
   Stirred for the grief they could not else assuage;
"*Because* it cannot help,"—he said,—"I weep."

UNDERTOW.

It is a boon for which to render praise
  Beyond our wont, that Heaven the power imparts
  To hide away our festering griefs and smarts,
And shut us safe from all intrusive gaze.
  For oft-times when the impassive brow is still,
  And the hoarse murmurs of the world sink low,
The inward ear is deafened by the flow
  Of whirling maelstroms whose strong eddies fill
  The soul with tempest-wrack: And then to wear
To eyes wherein no soft responses dwell,
  A face of tidal quiet that shall bear
  No ripple of undercurrents, is surely well.
Who would that even the lovingest heart should know
The secret springs of many an hour of woe?

IF.

—hic tandem felicis—

AND did the dumb and ghastly solitude,
   The pale, perpetual quiet of the grave,
   Wherein retributive passions cease to rave,
Hush that tumultuous spirit's rankling mood,
Till all its stormy riot was subdued,
   And the salt wretchedness it sought to brave,
   Ebbed into silence, a spent, wintry wave?
Yea,—if so be the calm did but include
Final redemption from the woeful strife
   In which he vanquisht sank;—if mercy's kiss
   Of reconcilement sealed his lips before
The bitter culmination of his life, -
   Then found he, through that open grave, a door
That at the last, hath let him into bliss.

GOD'S PATIENCE.

Of all the attributes whose starry rays
   Converge and centre in one focal light
   Of luminous glory such as angels' sight
Can only look on with a blench'd amaze,
   None crowns the brow of God with purer blaze,
Nor lifts His grandeur to more infinite height,
Than His exhaustless patience. Let us praise
With wondering hearts, this strangest, tenderest grace,
   Remembering awe-struck, that the avenging rod
Of justice must have fallen, and mercy's plan
   Been frustrate, had not Patience stood between,
   Divinely meek: And let us learn that man,
Toiling, enduring, pleading,—calm, serene,
For those who scorn and slight, is likest God.

THE SHADOW.

It comes betwixt me and the amethyst
   Of yon far mountain's billowy range;—the sky,
Mild with sunsetting calmness, to my eye
   Is curtained ever by its haunting mist:
And oftentimes when some dear brow I've kissed,
My lips grow tremulous as it sweeps me by,
With stress of overmastering agony
   That faith and reason all in vain resist.
It blurs my fairest books; it dims the page
   Of the divinest lore; and on my tongue
The broken prayer that inward strength would crave,
   Dissolves in sobs no soothing can assuage:
And this penumbral gloom,—this heart-cloud flung
Around me is, the memory of a grave.

FAILURE.

NEVER on any of God's creatures shone
    A cheerier sunshine than on us to-day!
    Nature's most priceless gifts,—her rich array,
Soft air, pure sky, green earth and mountain zone,
Are in fee-simple, each and all our own,
    As freely as yonder oriole's on the spray
    Of out-bloom'd lilac there, who trills away
His heart in rapture, though his spring be flown.
Our quick blood tingles zestfully; the fair,
    Persistent augury of hope is heard;
The burden'd spirit uplifts with lithe rebound;
    All life without, within defies despair;
Yet *"Failure,—Failure,"*—still is sighed around:
—Go to!—we will not listen to the word!

NON DOLET.

WHEN downfall and disaster sore beset
   The Roman Arria,—yielding to the tide
   Of ills that overwhelmed on every side,
With unheroic heart that could forget
'Twas cowardice to die,—she dared and met
   The easier fate, and luring, sought to hide
   For her belovéd's sake (true woman yet!)
The inward anguish with a wifely pride.
Not so our Southern Arria:—In the face
Of deadlier woes, she dared to live, and wring
   Hope out of havoc: till the brave control,
   Pathetic courage and most tender grace
Of her "*non dolet*," nerved her husband's soul,
Won him to life, and dulled even failure's sting.

RELIGIOUS PIECES.

RABBONI.

I.

Of all the nights of most mysterious dread,
  This elded earth hath known, none matched in gloom
That crucifixion night when Christ lay dead,
  —Sealed up in Joseph's tomb!

II.

No faith that rose sublime above the pain,
  Remembered in its anguish what He said;
"After three days, and I shall rise again,"—
  Their hopeless hearts were dead.

III.

Throughout that ghastly "Preparation-Day,"
  How had the stricken mother dragged her breath!
—Like all of Adam born, her God-given lay
  Beneath the doom of death.

IV.

The prophecy she nursed through pondering years
  Of apprehension, now had found its whole
Fulfillment, infinite beyond her fears,
      —The sword *had* pierced her soul!

V.

The vehement tears of Peter well might flow,
  Mixed with the wormwood of repentant shame;
Now would he yield his life thrice told, if so
      He might confess the name

VI.

He had denied with curses. Fruitless were
  The keen remorses now, the gnawing smart;
A heavier stone than sealed the sepulchre
      Was rolled above his heart.

VII.

Surprise and grief and baffled hopes sufficed
  To rush as seas their souls and God between;
Yet none of all had mourned the buried Christ,
      As Mary Magdalene.

VIII.

When all condemned,—He bade her live again,
  When all were hard,—His pity poured above

Her penitent spirit, healed it, cleansed its stain,
    And made it pure with love.

IX.

And she had broken all her costliest store
  O'er Him whose tenderness, so new, so rare,
Stood like a strong, white angel evermore
    'Twixt her and mad despair.

X.

And He was dead!—Her peace had died with Him!
  The dæmons who had fled at His control,
With seven-fold chains within their dungeons dim,
    Would henceforth bind her soul.

XI.

—How slowly crept the Sabbath's endless week!
  What aching vigils watched the lingering day,
When she might stagger through the dark and seek
    The garden where He lay!

XII.

And when she thrid her way to meet the dawn,
  And found the gates unbarred,—a grieving moan
Brake from her lips—"Who,"—for her strength was
    gone,—
        "Will roll away the stone?"

XIII.

She held no other thought, no hope but this;
   To look,—to touch the sacred flesh once more,—
Handle the spices with adoring kiss,
      And help to wind Him o'er

XIV.

With the fair linen Joseph had prepared,—
   Lift reverently the wounded hands and feet,
And gaze, awe-blinded, on the features bared,
      And drink the last, most sweet,

XV.

Divine illusion of His presence there;
   And then, the embalming done, with one low cry
Of utmost, unappeasable despair,
      Seek out her home, and die.

XVI.

Lo! the black square that showed the opened tomb!
   She sprang,—she entered unafraid,—and swept
Her arms outstretching, groping through the gloom,
      To touch Him where He slept.

XVII.

Her trembling fingers grasped the raiment cold,
   Pungent with aloes, lying where He lay:

She smoothed her hands above it, fold by fold,
   —Her Lord was stolen away!—

XVIII.

And others came anon, who wept Him sore,
  —Simon and John, the women pale and spent
With fearful watchings; wondering more and more,
    They questioned, gazed,—and went.

XIX.

Not thus did Mary. Though the lingering gloom
  Pearled into brightness, and the city's stir
Came floating upward to the garden tomb,
    There was no dawn for her:

XX.

No room for faintest hopes, nor utmost fears;
  For when she sobbing stooped and saw the twain
White-clothen angels, through her falling tears,   .
    Sit where her Lord had lain,—

XXI.

And ask,—"Why weepest thou?"—there brake no cry,
  But she with deaden'd calm her answer made:
"Because they have taken away my Lord, and I
    Know not where He is laid."

XXII.

—Was it a step upon the dewy grass?
　　Was it a garment rustled by the wind?
Did some husht breathing o'er her senses pass,
　　　　And draw her looks behind?

XXIII.

She turned and saw—the very Lord she sought,—
　　Jesus, the newly-risen! . . . but no surprise
Held her astound and rooted to the spot;
　　　　Her film'd and holden eyes

XXIV.

Had only vision for the swathéd form;
　　Nor from her mantle lifted she her face,
Nor marvelled that the gardener's voice should warm
　　　　With pity at her case;—

XXV.

Till sprang the sudden thought, "If *he* should know:—"
　　And then she turned full quickly: "Sir, I pray,
Tell me where thou hast borne Him, that I may go
　　　　And take Him thence away."

XXVI.

The resurrection-morning's broadening blaze
　　Shot up behind, and clear before her sight,

Centered on Jesus its transfiguring rays,
    And haloed Him with light.

XXVII.

"*Mary!*"—The measureless pathos was the same
    As when her Lord had said—"Thou art forgiven:"
Had He, for comfort, named her by her name
    Out from the height of heaven?

XXVIII.

She looked aloft,—she listened, turned and gazed;
    A revelation flashed across her brow;
One moment,—and she prostrate fell, amazed,—
    "*Rabboni!—It is Thou!*"

THE CHILD JESUS.

I.

ALL placid and lonely the village
   Of Nazareth slept on the plain;
No husbandman toiled at the tillage,
   Nor reaped the ripe ears of the grain:
No vine-dressers wrought at their labors,
   Nor passed with their pruning-hooks by:
The slopes were as silent as Tabor's,
   And Tabor was still as the sky.

II.

No voices of innocent riot
   In market-place, hostel or hut:
The hum of the craftsman was quiet,
   The door of the synagogue shut.
No *Alephs* and *Beths* were heard swelling
   From the school of the scribe, by the wall;
And Joseph-the-carpenter's dwelling
   Was hushed as the publican's stall.

III.

'Twas the week of the Passover: only
　The agéd, the sickly, the blind,
The tottering children and lonely
　Young mothers, had tarried behind.
To the sacredest Feast of the nation,
　Through the paths that their fathers had trod,
All others with paschal oblation
　Had gone to the City of God.

IV.

And Mary,—to every beholder,
　Her face toucht with wistfulest dole,
(Remembering what Simeon had told her
　Of the sword that should pierce through her soul,—)
With faith yet too steadfast to falter,
　Though sorely with mysteries tried,
Midst the worshippers stood at the altar,
　With Jesus the child by her side.

V.

The seven days' festival ended,—
　Rites finished for people and priest,
The throngs from the Temple descended,
　And homeward set face from the Feast.
And neighbor held converse with neighbor,
　Unwonted and simple and free,

As northward they journeyed toward Tabor,
  Or westward they turned to the sea.

VI.

But not till the night-dews were falling,
  Did Mary, oft questioning, find,
As children to children were calling,
  That Jesus had lingered behind.
He vex her?—the mother that bore Him?
  —Or veiled it some portent or sign?
For oft had she trembled before Him,—
  Her human too near His divine.

VII.

She sought midst her kinsfolk, whose pity
  Grew tender to look on her grief:
Then back through the streets of the city
  She hastened, yet found not relief.
Thus searching, a marvellous story
  Her ear and her senses beguiled;
—"The Rabbis, grey-bearded and hoary,
  In the Temple are taught by a child."

VIII.

O, marvel of womanly weakness!
  She finds Him:—fears, sorrows subside,
And Mary, the angel of meekness,
  In petulance pauses to chide:

—" Son, wherefore thus tarry to gather
  About Thee the curious throng,
Unheeding the while, that Thy father
  And I have been seeking Thee long?"

IX.

A look so reproachfully tender,
  It awed while it melted her eye,
He cast, as He hastened to render
  Subjection and filial reply:
—"Nay,—wherefore perplexed and pursuing?
  Dost *thou* too, my mother, forget,
And wist not the Son must be doing
  The work that His Father hath set?"

SUPPER AT BETHANY.

AND now the even-tide had come, and Jesus' blessèd feet
Ached with the long day's ceaseless toil within the scorching street.

The Temple's topmost pinnacle held fast a sunbeam yet,
While grey the shadows hung around the groves of Olivet.

"Master, the hour wears late; behold, the sun hath left the west,
The thronging crowds have prest Thee sore, and Thou hast need of rest.

"The Twelve return from court and lane, and all their teachings cease;
Beseech Thee, leave these noisy ways, and go apart for peace."

With urgency thus Peter spake as the hot streets grew
    dim;
And Jesus knew each word was said through anxious
    care for Him.

So out beyond the gates they went,—the Master
    walked before,
And stars shone through the olives ere they paused
    at Martha's door.

Instant her earnest zeal was fired; with tumult of
    accord
Her toucht heart sprang with haste to yield due honor
    to her Lord.

And through the quiet-order'd house is strange, un-
    wonted stir;
—The Master, spent and travail-worn, hath deigned
    to come to her.

So tired He seems, that to and fro she flies with
    quick command;
And as she speeds the hurrying meal, she misses
    Mary's hand.

"What!—following Him with questionings still,—there,
    sitting at His feet,
When tasked with teachings, He is faint for lack of
    food to eat?

"Lord, for Thy needful earthly meat hast Thou so little care?
Nay, bid my sister come and help, that we for Thee prepare."

Amid His parables He paused to hearken while she spake,
And Mary's startled, down-dropt face a lowlier look did take.

And Jesus said, while tender love ran infinite through each word,
(He knew that fretted heart for *Him* with fervid zeal was stirred:)

"Ah, Martha, Martha, many things thy daily comfort vex,
And troubles manifold distract, and cumbering cares perplex:

"But one thing only needful is, and verily I say,
Mary hath chosen that better part which none shall take away."

EVEN SO, FATHER.

WHEN from the central throne on which the eyes
Of seraphim could only avail to look
With half-uplifted lids and clouding wings
Raised shieldingly betwixt them and God's face,—
The Christ descended,—wonder throbbed through heaven.
Unblenched their strong, far-piercing sight could bear
The near, full gaze upon the countless suns
That met them in their circling sweep through space,
But from *His* glory, they shrank dazzled, blind.
Then how should man, poor atom of a day,
Endure the perilous brightness, and yet live?

Not even angelic nature might conceive
Such abnegation,—such a putting off
Of Godhead splendors,—such an humbling down
Of pure Divinity's sovereign attributes,
That the clay vessel of humanity
Could hold concentrate in its finite sphere

Omniscience that out-flashed the bournless verge
Of God's grand universe. And when they looked
To see Him burst with undisputed sway
Upon that little, distant speck in space
Where the rebellious dwelt, whose impotence
Should shrivel awe-struck before Him,—who shall
    recount
Their dumb bewilderment, as back the host
Came rapid with the tidings,—They had left
The Son of God, a babe in swaddling-bands!

With questioning gaze intense, they bent to read
The mystery's meaning. They beheld the child,
A human sleeper on a human breast,
With new-found sense of that Omnipotence
That thus could narrow and shut itself behind
A mask of flesh: and more the amazement grew
That she,—a mortal,—dared to press those hands
With such familiar love, when *they* had hung
Back from His touch in heaven.

                    Through all His years
Of Nazareth toil,—of goings to and fro
Up to Jerusalem's paschal feasts, they watched,
Panting to pierce the yet unlifted veil.
And when the hour of His forth-setting came,
They but beheld humiliation still.
Not from the ranks of venerable state,—

Not from the porches of the vaunted schools,—
Not from the lineage of inspired souls
Whose prescience far outran the generation
That knew them not,—not from the lordly race,
Affluent of wisdom, lofty-doing or power,—
Saw they Him choose the fitting instruments
Wherewith to work His vast accomplishments.
But He did take Him poor, ignoble men,
(As calendared in earthly registry,)
And put into their stammering, untaught lips,
Words that the high-born angels dared not use.

Foul dæmons that had ravined unafraid
Over this marred creation,—thrusting forth
Their hissing insolence in the very front
Of Heaven's pure ministrants, they marvelled to see
Confounded shrink away, when these weak men
Gave utterance to their exorcising spell,
And spake the name of Jesus. They beheld
Fierce hearts that scouted God and mocked His love,
Break and grow soft and heave with aspirations
Saintly as even their own: And a fresh thought
Of that stupendous power that with such helps,
Could work such ends, begat in them new joy.

And when they heard the voice of Christ Himself
Uplifted in that lone Judean vale,
In audible thanksgiving and praise,—more rapt,

They bent and listened still :
                    "I thank thee, Father,
Lord of the heaven and earth, that Thou hast hid
Thy wisdom from the wise and prudent, and hast
Revealed it unto babes like these: Even so
Father,—since thus 'tis good within Thy sight."

As died the utterance on those sacred lips,
The listeners caught it up in glad amaze,
And bore it heavenward, ever murmuring,
As o'er the Atonement's yet unfolded plan
They mused in mute astonishment,—"Even so
Father,—since thus it seemeth good to Thee !"

THE SEARCH OF THE SAGES.

I.

ALL night upon their lofty tower,
  With upturned brow and straining eye,
The Persian Sages watched each hour
  Of the brief, orient dusk go by:
Yet still that unfamiliar star,
Mysteriously near, yet far,
Prevailing with such steadfast blaze
Above Orion's belted rays,
Or mellower Pleiades, was there,
  Unheralded, unnamed, unknown:
  No Chaldees' chart its place had shown
In the broad heavens; and yet how rare
Its radiance was!—how crystal fair!

II.

It did not set, like other stars,
  It did not melt away nor wane;

But steadier than the fiery Mars,
   Each night beheld it gleam again
In unshorn splendor. Was it sent,
Precursor of some strange event,
The gods would thus reveal to earth?
Did it presage some Princely birth,
   Some regnant sway that should extend
From south to north, from east to west,
O'er all the Islands of the Blest,
   Far as the sun his beams might send,
   Even to the world's remotest end?

III.

Thus grew the thought:—"It must be so!
   The star tends westward, as we see;
The sacred Hierarchs bid us go
   And seek the new-born Sovereignty.
Nor sent on embassage so grand,
Dare we depart with empty hand:
But of our costliest, richest things
'Tis meet we bear this King of kings,
   Right royal offerings,—Uphaz' gold,
The myrrh of Saba, spices sweet,
To lay, for homage at His feet,
   Whose empire vast and manifold,
   Such mighty augury hath foretold."

IV.

So, forth upon their heaven-sent way,
　The Sages journeyed long and far,
With eyes updrawn to watch the ray
　That glittered from their pilot star.
And when meridian suns on high
Drowned its new sparkle from the sky,
Trustful, they paused within their tent,
Until the eclipsing glory went
Down goldenly beneath the plain;
　And then with hope half-touched with fear,
　They looked aloft, and fixt and clear,
Each eve, amid the twilight's wane,
They hailed their mystic guide again.

V.

With thirsty eyes its beams they quaffed,
　And followed at its silent call,
Until it dropt a crystal shaft
　Right over Bethlehem's village wall.
They marvelled wherefore there should be
No stir of royal pageantry;
They looked to see the palace light,
They deemed would daze the vulgar sight;
Yet strangely urged, they onward passed
Through careless throngs, and reached at last

A clay-built shed o'er which their guide
   Stood still. A wide-eyed, dumb amaze
One instant held them: but the rays
   Shot straight the litter'd straw beside.
Then,—mute before the mystery
   Unfathomable, in meekness they
Entered with offerings, worship, praise,
   And owned the Sovereignty that lay
Swathed in our weak humanity,
A babe upon a woman's knee.

THE YOUNG RULER'S QUESTION.

He had riches and ease and honor,
    And never a Jewish boy
Had passed on the banks of Jordan
    A tenderer youth of joy.

He had houses and fields and vineyards,
    And blessings of all degree;
None had a fairer portion
    In beautiful Galilee.

Whatever this world could offer
    Of pure and innocent bliss,
Whatever his nature needed
    Of goodliest gifts, was his.

He had felt no weary longings,—
    No wants that were unsupplied;
Upright and just and noble,
    His spirit was satisfied.

Only one thought had power
   Ever a cloud to cast:
—Joy, to be wholly perfect,
   Must be a joy *to last:*

And he knew that his own was fleeting;
   For he read in the sacred Psalm,
That man must fade as a flower,
   And it sometimes marred his calm.

He turned to the holy Prophets,
   Security thence to draw;
And he listened to Moses' teachings,
   And he strove to keep the Law.

He tithed his anise and cummin,
   He tithed his mint and rue:
He *knew* he had earth's best treasures,—
   He *hoped* he had heaven's too.

—In the mart of a busy city
   It came to pass, one day,
That a throng of curious people
   Was choking the narrow way;

All pressing with upturned faces,
   Eager to hear and see

The miracle-working Rabbi
 Who had come to Galilee.

—"Now, verily, what will it profit
 A man, though he gain the whole
Of the world, with its utmost glory,
 If yet he should lose his soul?

"Come unto me, ye weary—"
 It dropped on the passing ear
Of the young and happy Ruler,
 For he could not choose but hear.

He did not pause to listen
 As he skirted the crowd, but went
Homeward athwart the city,
 Wrapped in his sweet content.

Yet ever and oft, the Teacher
 Rose to his inward eye;
Over and over the question
 Waited his heart's reply.

—Bliss that should be eternal,
 —Pleasures that could not cloy:
These were the very blessings
 Needed to crown his joy!

Again through the palm-girt highways,
  When noontide's sultry flame
Was searing the happy vineyards,
  The wonderful Teacher came.

And the Ruler hailed His coming;
  For harvest or vintage cheer
Never had silenced the question
  That troubled his restless ear.

Hastening, he sought the Prophet
  Whose words had wrought the strife:
—"What shall I do, good Master,
  To inherit eternal life?"

As he kneeled so young and guileless,
  Single in aim and art,—
Jesus, beholding him, loved him,
  Though He read his inmost heart.

And he answered and said, as gently
  As father would say to son:
—"Thou knowest the Ten Commandments;"
  And he spake them one by one.

A look that was half reproachful
  The eye of the Saviour met:

—"All these I have kept from childhood;
　　Good Master, what lack I yet?"

And Jesus, beholding him, loved him,
　　And a human sympathy stole,
As He gazed on the earnest pleader,
　　Deep into His sacred soul.

All blessings this life could bring him
　　Even now were his, He knew;
But he coveted both possessions,—
　　The earthly and heavenly too.

Never diviner pity
　　Melted the mournful eye,
Never a tearfuler yearning,
　　Than softened the firm reply:

"Only one thing thou lackest;
　　Forego thy heritage here,
All of thy stored abundance,
　　Everything heart holds dear:

"Choose thee between the blessings,
　　This, or the life to be:
Thou shalt have treasure in heaven,
　　If thou wilt follow me!"

THE YOUNG RULER'S QUESTION.

A sudden, surprised dejection
    Flooded the lifted face,
Doubting and disappointment
    Darkened the wistful gaze.

Verily, this was a doctrine
    Hard for the flesh and sore;
This was a self-denying
    Never conceived before!

Had there been half required,
    Then he might heed the call:
Dignities, loves, possessions,—
    How could he yield them all?

Bitter the stern exaction
    Fell on his heart that day;
And wavering,—wishing,—choosing,—
    He sorrowfully went away.

—Ye who have read and marvelled
    That Jesus, who loved him so,
Should let him depart unhindered,—
    Will ye, like the Ruler, go?

Ponder the solemn question
    Deep in each conscience set,

Asking in soulfelt earnest,
"Master, what lack I yet?"

Choose ye, as every seeker
Who findeth Him truly doth,
—Earthly, or heavenly treasure;
For ye cannot inherit both.

Ye may be near the kingdom,—
Nearer than any know;
And Jesus may love and pity,
And yet,—*He may let you go!*

READY.

I would be ready, Lord,
  My house in order set,
None of the work Thou gavest me
  To do, unfinished yet.

I would be watching, Lord,
  With lamp well-trimmed and clear,
Quick to throw open wide the door,
  What time Thou drawest near.

I would be waiting, Lord,
  Because I cannot know
If in the night or morning watch,
  I may be called to go.

I would be working, Lord,
  Each day, each hour for Thee;
Assured that thus I wait Thee well,
  Whene'er Thy coming be.

I would be living, Lord,
    As ever in Thine eye;
For whoso lives the holiest life,
    Is fittest far to die.

THE TWO MITES.

"To-day is the day of oblation,
    And the people with one accord
Are bringing their free-will offerings
    To the treasury of the Lord.

"With tithings and consecrations
    The faithful are hastening thence;
The rich with their sanctuary shekels,
    The poor with their hard-earn'd pence.

"'Honor the Lord with thy substance,'—
    (These are the words divine,)
'And thy barns shall be filled with plenty,
    Thy presses shall burst with wine.'

"To *me* is the precept spoken?
    —Yea, even to me, who am
An heir and a child of promise,
    A daughter of Abraham.

THE TWO MITES.

"Yet in my need and straitness,
    Hardly bestead to live,
Desolate, lonely, widowed,
    What have I left to give?

"Yet there is quiet solace
    To feel that *he* cannot know,
How the dole he left in the coffer
    Failed me so long ago.

"And now I am hoarding in it
    Only two mites, my all;
—Two mites which make but a farthing,
    And that is a gift so small!

"So small when I count the blessings,
    The marvellous, rich reward
I have found in His sacred service,—
    So little to bring my Lord!

"Yet naught of *our* gifts He needeth,
    Whose plenitude boundless is:
The corn, the wine and the olives,
    The flocks and the herds are His.

"So among the golden talents,
    I will hide my mites, and pray

That He who feedeth the sparrows,
　Will keep me in mind to-day.

"He knoweth I blush to offer
　My penury's straiten'd store;
But I'll give myself with my farthing,
　And then He will count it more."

She wist not that Christ was watching,
　As she offered her alms so small;
She heard not His commendation,
　—"She hath given, yea, more than all."

For the prayer in which she wrapped it
　Outweighed the treasury's gold;
And the mites which made but a farthing,
　Have yielded a million-fold.

THE SYMPATHY OF JESUS.

I.

Who that hath been sore smitten,—who
   That ever sobbed one wordless moan
On some warm bosom, fond and true,
   Some sorrowing bosom, like our own,
And felt how much those lips close-prest,
   That hand close-claspt, could hush our fears,—
Can turn to Jesus' tenderer breast
   Nor know the chasten'd bliss of tears!

II.

The earthly heart on which we lean
   May have its separate griefs to bear,
A cross undreamed-of, woes unseen,
   Wounds that we lacerate unaware:
Its staggering strength may scarce sustain
   The burden of its own distress,
And still we heap our cumbering pain,
   Unconscious how the weight may press.

III.

But He whose human feet have trod
  All paths of trial, He who knew
No sympathy but that of God,
  Though linked with flesh that craved it too,—
Yearns with us in our needs, our dreads,
  And mindful of our feeble frame,
Holds to His heart our throbbing heads
  With love that hath no mortal name.

IV.

We know that on the throne of thrones,
  He wears our lowly nature still;
We know that through the loftiest tones
  With which adoring seraphs thrill,
He bends the faintest prayer to hear,
  Though only sighs our anguish tell:
That sobbing voice falls on His ear
  Sweeter than Gabriel's ever fell!

V.

Then, desolate spirit,—take the grief
  Thou to no mortal canst disclose,
And He will give thee sure relief,
  Touched with the feeling of thy woes:

And thou shalt learn how all complete,
　How far above earth's purest bliss,
How passing more than human-sweet,
　The sympathy of Jesus is!

THE LITTLE PILGRIMS.

Soiled with the dust of travel,
    Weary with wandering late,
Two little lagging pilgrims
    Paused at the castle gate.

Sorely their feet had stumbled,
    Often they'd gone astray
After the fruits and blossoms
    Scattered along their way.

Many an hour they'd loitered
    Carelessly on:—yet who,
Seeing the path was rugged,
    Would not have loitered too?

Never a hand to check them,
    Never a smile to cheer;
Shadowy memories only
    Filling the childish ear.

Once as they idly dallied,
　　Scallop and staff thrown by,
Over them dropt a whisper
　　Out of the silent sky.

Up from their play they started,
　　Wetted in haste their lips,
Girded themselves for travel,
　　Shouldered their scanty scrips;

Speeding as if belated
　　Hurriedly on their way,
Softly the younger asking,
　　"What did our mother say?"

"'*Knock and it shall be opened:*'
　　Ah, if the whisper stirs
Both of our hearts so,—surely,
　　Surely the voice *was* hers!

"Cannot you mind her saying
　　Stretching her arms to go,—
'I will be with you nearer,
　　Oftener than you know?

"'Out of the skies I'll call you,
　　Tenderly leaning through;

—Listen, with faces, darlings,
  Lifted toward the blue.

"'*Knock and it shall be opened,
  Seek and I know you'll find:*
These are the words I'll whisper
  When you are left behind.'

"So,—I have heard her, brother,
  When we have tarried late,
Calling us 'little pilgrims,'
  Bidding us seek the gate;

"Telling us 'tis the pathway
  Out of this world of sin;
Yonder,—I see the wicket,
  Come, let us enter in."

TEMPLE-SERVICE.

I.

I TURN to Thee!—My heart hath been
  A desecrated shrine,
And on its holiest altar, where
  Should burn the flame divine,
Strange fire consumed a sacrifice
  I made not wholly Thine.

II.

I knelt with offerings in my hands,
  And ashes on my brow,
While yet divided worship breathed
  In every prayer and vow;
—To gods beyond the outer courts
  My soul had dared to bow.

III.

Cleanse Thou the temple, Great High Priest,
  Anoint its altar-stone;

The blood that wet Thy wounded hands,
  Can purge, restore, atone;
And be each pure oblation sealed
  Henceforth to God alone.

IV.

Within Thy golden censer laid,
  Bear heavenward I implore,
The bruis'd frankincense and the myrrh,
  The tears and prayers I pour;
Nor let irreverent rites profane
  Thy hallowed service more!

www.ingramcontent.com/pod-product-compliance
Lightning Source LLC
Chambersburg PA
CBHW031906220426
43663CB00006B/787